PLANNING

Means success.

Graeme Smith

PUBLISHED ON AMAZON.com
by
LABYRINTH BOOKS

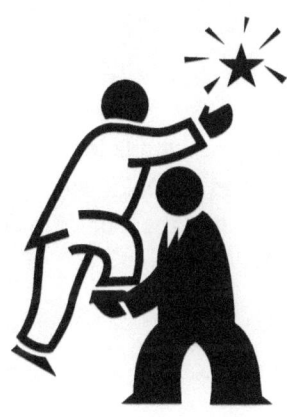

DEDICATION:

This book is dedicated to my family.

Hele-ly (Ly).
my wife:

Ingrid.
our daughter:

Marie.
my former wife:

Fiona, Natalie and Michael
our children:

Georgie
Michael's wife:

Pearl, Kiki and Martha.
their children:

They have had to put up with me for many years and I thank them for that.
I hope this book gives them an insight into what has occupied me.
All have done worthwhile and interesting things in the absence of my help.
I congratulate them for their achievements.

HOW TO USE THIS BOOK.

First think - then do.
Usually people don't think through things to the level they need to.
Because of that, they have projects instead of tasks on their "to do" list.
That leads to procrastination as it hasn't been broken down to a task level.

So go through your book once to understand it.
Go through it again.

Then start at the idea you would like to implement first.
Make notes of the steps you will need to take and the resources required.
Use these notes to create a step by step system for implementing the guide.
Often you will not refer to the original, once you've created **YOUR** system.

The first question to ask and answer is "Why is this being done?"
How does this align with where you want to get to?
What are the strategic implications of doing this?
Does this fit with getting to your goal in the shortest and fastest time?
What would it be like if it were totally successful?
Define it - what is success for this project and how will you know?

Now brainstorm all the tasks that are involved in your project.
It's important not to go linear too fast with this.
By linear, I mean step one, step two, step three, and step four.
You end up cutting off options.
As you plan step one, two, three, there is a specific step that might be four.
Start steps too quickly, other ways for one, two and three may not appear.

The first third of any brainstorming session is really easy.
Just come up with lots of ideas.
The second third is challenging - go through ideas and see where they lead.
Then push yourself to think a little bit outside the box.
That's often where the big idea is!
That's where the most powerful way of getting a project done fastest - is.

Most people never get to that level and short-change themselves.
Then their project takes longer and they also set up to procrastinate.
This final brainstorming part of the equation is incredibly important.

Once fully brainstormed put your options into a linear sequence.
Then you can figure out what you've overlooked.
Everything becomes obvious as you get your tasks in order.
Now add missing steps and you have laid out your task list for this project.

When you've organized the tasks into a linear process decide:
What things can you start immediately?
What can be started that are not dependent on what occurred before them?
Obviously that is step one.
There might be step five, six or twenty that don't rely on anything else to do.
You can get started on them right away too.

Now use a folder.
Write things you think of at the time and also cross off things as you do them.
Add in stuff that is relevant from time to time.

PLAN FOR SUCCESS.

INDEX: PLANNING

SUPPORT:

The International Artist magazine – international magazine for artists

The Australian Artist magazine – magazine for artists

Clipping Path Universe – for photo-shop editing

Cherri Computers – for computer hardware, software and printers.

1. GETTING STARTED.

Reviewed by Alfred Memelink - (Wellington, New Zealand)

1. Have you ever waited for inspiration?

Did you find that you had to wait for a long time?
Here's how I discovered how to avoid the start stopping me!

One evening I arrived for my art class to find I was the only one there!
Our lecturer for this particular class didn't ever have much to say.
That's when he was there **BUT** he wasn't there.
My fellow class members followed his pattern too, for this was a night class.

I decided not to waste my time.
I looked at my blank canvas and didn't know what to do.
The start certainly had me stopped.
I was almost three years through the four year course.

But I did not know what to do.
Have you had this feeling?
It was totally unexpected.
I now realize that teachers and lecturers usually provide the starting point.

Students are not in the situation that I found myself.
After quite a while, I looked at my paints and noticed a tube of Indian Red.
I decided that I'd use that - it's a colour I dislike.
If I was going to waste some paint it may as well be a colour like that.
So I mixed Indian red with turps, still with no real thought about what to do.
Then just because the paint was runny, I flicked some onto the canvas.
I splashed some more and still further splashes followed the first ones.
I looked at the canvas for a while, all covered with splashes of Indian red.
It was a bit like an Indian red 'Jackson Pollock' painting.

Still not knowing what to do, I decided to join up the dots and splashes.
After a while, I looked again at the canvas, all covered with irregular shapes.
But I was no further ahead in working out what to do.

More speculation led me to the idea I could colour-in some shapes.
Then I squeezed out some white paint and blocked-in several of the shapes.
I used various white and Indian red mixtures and was quite busy doing this.
Eventually I finished and had another look at what I had done.

Even though I didn't know what to do, I had done something.
It was an abstract painting and I was reasonably pleased with the result.
Even though I had not anticipated that before starting.

AND no longer does the start stop me.
It doesn't matter what you do at the start, as long as you do something.
It can even be quite random, as my first self-discovered start was.
That doesn't necessarily have to be the case though.

There is no need to wait for inspiration - just make a few marks.
Imagination cannot work on a blank surface, it needs help!

2. Let's put this lesson to some use!

Whenever you experience artist's block, do something, anything at all.
There is less preciousness attached to small works than larger ones.
So keep this exercise to about 35cm x 25cm maximum or even less.

It doesn't matter what you do at the start, as long as you do something.
It can even be quite random, just like my first self-discovered starts were.
There is no need to wait for inspiration - just make a few marks.
Your mind uses imagination which can't work on a blank surface.
It needs help but random starts don't necessarily have to be the case.

Just painting (anything in any way) is a powerful tool.
Do this regularly, even daily.
Make 5 or 10 or 20 experiments a part of your daily routine.
Take a leaf out of an athlete's program, train daily, or several times a day!
So now paint 200 or more (250 or even 300) of these small experiments.
The quality will improve, particularly if you don't worry about it at the time.
Naturally this improvement will not be at the start.
It will take some time before you notice the improvement, but it will happen!

At the very least you will learn what not to do and what won't work.
Knowing this takes you closer to what will work and what should be done.

Other people's standards are a barrier to finding your own way.
Your work is not relevant to what anyone else does - just do it!
If you do what you do, then that is your present level.
BUT at some point your standard will go past where it was previously.
Your standard is probably related to your style.
Keep improving and you'll set new standards.

Look back from time to time and see if you have improved.
You'll get a pleasant surprise because you consistently lift the bar higher.
AND you know you can always get better.
Then you'll be making every work your best.
Just **DON'T** think standard while you paint.
The more you do, the better you get, and the higher your standard becomes.

The small sizes will speed up production of 200+ studies.
Obviously framing 200 small works costs money - so **DON'T** frame them.
Because they aren't framed or sold it will **NOT** matter if they turn out or not.
Enjoy a no pressure relaxed attitude, with satisfying results from time to time.

What will become of all those experiments?
Nothing, save them if you like, those didn't work out might be important later.

A professional artist needs a detached view of their own works!
Here's where you can start developing that!
A professional artist knows they have to part with most of their best paintings.
You'll eventually accept this as part of being a professional artist.
You'll be able to do that for you'll know there **WILL** be more 'best' ones.
Thus you'll be less worried than the beginner who fears that there will not be.
Your 200+ experiments will help you realize the truth of this.

You will also commit ideas to your memory bank.
Looking at various experiments will refresh ideas beyond what is there.

3. But what about planning?

Planning is just the same process.
Plan because there's something you want to do.
There is an idea you want to develop OR there is something you want to try.
That's what having sincerity and integrity is about!
Any other reason and it will be hard to maintain motivation and enthusiasm.
Particularly in the long term as your career will be.

If you plan do you think everything step x step before doing anything?
Decide where you want to be, study where you are now and work out steps.
Many artists apply that thinking to their planning.

A report (Sydney 'Herald' 26th April, 2003) suggests a different way.
The article wasn't about artists, but golfers.
Successful professionals say golf is 95% mental.
But lesser golfers don't believe it.
So they pay professionals to teach how to hit the ball, stand properly, etc.
It's the same in our field isn't it?

The report was about research done at the University of Chicago.
Professional and amateur golfers were compared.
Brain activation of the two groups showed areas highly active in amateurs.
An area that co-ordinates sensory input with emotions, and another that controls cognition (thinking), movement co-ordination and voluntary movement, were highly active in the amateurs.
But **NOT** the professionals.

It was thought activity in amateurs took too much time and didn't focus.
They might have been more anxious about the shot than professional.
Too much data inhibits motor planning and performance.
Thus activating some areas of the brain.
The amateur thinks each shot is a new shot.
The professional knows they're the same as before already internalized.
Thus their game is mental, as they don't need to focus on physical aspects.

This is consistent with learned skills (the authors do not say this).
Professional golfers' skill means they do not need to focus on that aspect.
Their actions become almost automatic and they focus on other aspects.
Such things as pin placement, slope of the green etc.

You'll understand this better if I relate it to driving a car.
When learning to drive, everything has to be explained.

You think through the process of driving almost in words.
I'd better brake here, turn the indicator, now, and so on.
Eventually your skill levels improve and you become a better driver.
You don't need to talk your way through each step of the driving process.
You just do it and the better you get, the less you think (consciously anyway).
AND the faster you can respond to whatever circumstances that arise.

Imagine you have to actually talk your way through an intersection?
You'd have an accident for sure – just about every time!
Talking is too slow and an inefficient method for guiding actions.

But you don't drive without any thought at all, or you'd have accidents.
When people have become skilled drivers they internalize their thinking.
Their thinking is non-verbal, faster and more efficient than language thinking.

In many sports things happen very quickly, we can see the evidence.
The top batsman hooks the fast bowler to the fence, or the leading soccer
player angles the ball past the keeper into the top of the net, and so on.
None of these actions is accidental or unintended.
Yet the player couldn't think it through in words in time to perform the action.
When you drive the car it's exactly the same and in golf it's the same too.
In fact learning and applying any skill happens this way.

Think about a child learning to walk.
The child just does it, without concern for what might happen.
The child is unaware of the consequences of failure and thus unworried.
The pro golfer is also unworried and thus confident.
Confidence is the key.

Do you think everything out, step by step as you plan anything?
Perhaps you are being too careful with your career planning?
You are possibly frightened of making a mistake.
There's no such thing, only something you learn.
If you fear mistakes you'll never learn anything, you'll repeat what you know.
This is the amateur golfer way.

You learn to plan by planning.
You do not learn by someone telling you what to do.
Then you only learn they know what to do and if you get stuck you ask them.
There's nothing that beats "doing it yourself" as a way of learning to plan.

4. Do you have a career focus?

But what is a focus anyway?
It's the rationale behind the painting that is a focus.
But if there is no rationale then there is no focus.
Van Gogh's focus was what caused him to create the kind of works he did.

Volvo makes cars, but that's not the company's focus.
For a long time their focus has been safety.
Similarly BMW has focused on producing driving machines.
The difference in focus is why their cars are different.
It's also why they appeal to different segments of the car buying public.

In the business world this is known as market segmentation.
Any market (paintings, cars) can be broken into different segments.

There is no market segment bought by all people.
To say your focus is watercolour is not sufficient.
That's because there is competition from others who also do watercolours.
The position your watercolour is in someone's mind, competitors are not.
If yours are expensive then others are cheap.
If you are low priced then others are up-market.
If your watercolours are soft then others are precise and sharp.
Large works are contrasted to miniatures and light to dark.
Even amateur and professional works are in someone's mind as alternatives.

So you only need to plan for the market sector you want to be in.
A dominant seller may try to be 'all things to everybody'.
But that's different and likely to result in a loss of focus.
The risk is they become nothing special to anybody.
An artist working in a variety of mediums, styles and subjects runs this risk.
They are justifiably proud of what they can do.
They compete against artists who only paint abstract oils, or whatever.
This artist only sells successfully with no opposition like at their own gallery.

They really should decide which aspect of the market to focus on.
Then support it by, suitable pricing, framing, promotion and distribution.
That's what focus is about.
Not willing to walk away from a segment of business, you don't have focus?
Can you imagine a '$10,000, drive away with no more to pay' Rolls Royce?
If they did do such a thing what do you think might happen?

Where I live students study art when in their final years of high school.
The main practical component of their course is to create a major work.
In other words they spend a lot of time over a single work.

Thus they get the message that this is how an artist usually works.
BUT they are not really learning much.
Only whatever they find out by spending a lot of time over a single work.
If they painted 200 works in the same time they would learn 200 times more!

Learning anything as an adult is different from learning as a child.
We know what the end is like because we have seen what others can do.
We want to get there too, so we hurry.
A kid doesn't know any of that and explores their way to where they get.
It's a different attitude and it's how we should approach a career as an artist.

Hasten slowly and develop your focus as you go.
Does your art career have a focus?
Are pricing, framing, promotion and distribution methods are all appropriate?
Decide what you want and then stick to it!

When you have a focus to your career you know what to do.
You'll know what kind of gallery you are looking for or need to retain.
You'll also know what sort of research to do or what new works to produce.

No one can stay on top of all things.
An unfocused artist will try to achieve balance.
All things are treated as being of equal importance.
Attention is shifted to make sure there is a rationing of effort.
Imagine paying as much attention to painting the works as framing or selling?
And researching ideas, various non-artistic activities, and you get the idea.
Knowledge is rapidly expanding as well, so how do you keep up?

A focus can direct you towards areas most likely to be of benefit to you.
A focus is particularly useful in trying to stay on top of developments.
A focused artist will put most of their resources into their future.
Focus really does mean moving from yesterday's ideas to to-morrows.
They may still have to deal with works or activity from the past.

BUT a focused artist makes it obvious they are not in any future plans.
In the short term you may need to deal with old works in an efficient way.
This could even mean moving them on at a discount.
That should not distract from putting most attention on to-morrow's focus.
Most artists tend to think like this, but do not really do it?

If you keep doing what you're doing, you keep getting what you've got.
Actually if you keep doing what you're doing, you'll get **WORSE** results!

But you can't change direction when there is no direction.
Focus is an ever-expanding mountain of knowledge and you are an expert.
You'll automatically put most effort, and dollars, where there might be results.

Best is have an inefficient, powerfully focused market-oriented career.
Than try to cover all bases and be efficient but inflexible.

Your logo is a symbol for your identity.
The logo is the most important ingredient of your identity, your focus.
Your signature is your logo.

5. Is your focus your future?

Your primary task is to work towards your future goals, so they happen.
Day to day things should be secondary.
You do have to manage your day to day activities.
BUT if that's all you do then your hopes and aspirations are left to chance.
Surely not good enough!

Make a prediction about your future.
Then take specific steps so it happens!
As already mentioned many years ago, Volvo selected 'safety' as a focus.
They predicted their future and the direction the industry would follow.
They also decided how their present (then) activities would be carried out.

Deciding about where you want to head is not just wishful thinking.
Look at what you are doing to-day.
What single service, product, or idea is your best hope for the future?
That becomes the basis for your future.
It's that simple!
It's also hard.

The hard part is making a right selection from different things you do.
It's hard because you really won't know you're right until time has passed.
By then it's probably too late to return to one of the previous options.
Never-the-less this is what you must do.
BUT as time goes there is an upward spiral supporting the original decision.
Your focus will allow you to develop in ways not previously for-seen.

A common scenario concerns which media you should use.
At an early career stage you'll use a variety as you explore and discover.
This is a learning, or student, phase and is important.
Then you make a professional decision about which media is your specialty.
It doesn't really matter, just so long as you enjoy it.
You spend extra time using this media and you'll get to know and do more.
Particularly compared with those who divide their time with different media.
The same kinds of comments apply to subject or style specializations too.

Such a decision can have short term penalties!
You now only enter in oil painting competition so won't win watercolor prizes.
Some people want your watercolors and won't buy your oils, too.
BUT the longer you follow a focus, the less important such penalties will be.

You'll be increasingly sought out for what you do, do.
It's much better to be really good at something than average at many things.
This is particularly true in the art business.
If you don't focus on something you may have a future which is nothing!

2. OVERCOMING OBSTACLES.

Reviewed by Victoria Dickinson - (Portland, Maine)
1. One of the toughest obstacle courses in the world.
2. What you really need to do now is prepare a career plan.
3. Nothing happens unless you do something.

1. One of the toughest obstacle courses in the world.

It is 10-12 miles and 3-hours long.
Jump off a 15 foot plank into icy cold water and swim to the next obstacle.
Run and crawl through trenches of mud.
Along the way you crawl underneath a barbed wire only 8" off the ground.

At a point you must grab a huge log and then hike up a ski slope with it.
Sprint through a field of wires, some of which carry a 10,000 volt shock.
Another part of the course you crawl over mud and rocks that shock you.
Then run through kerosene-soaked straw where flames are up to 4 feet high.
At some obstacles you wonder why anyone willingly subject to such torture!
This is designed by the British Special Forces.

Why would you want to continue struggling in your art career?
If you suffer from a lack of income because of the obstacles in your way!
It's no easier than the British Special Forces challenge.
Why not just remove the obstacles?
Your career doesn't have to be an obstacle course.
Taking away obstacles makes it much easier (and faster) to be successful.
You'd know how to avoid obstacles you'd stop running into roadblocks.
No longer would you continue to do things which are unproductive.

Remove the obstacles by doing some career planning.
It's an opportunity to remove barriers to people buying your works or classes.
Albert Einstein wrote:
"Everything should be made as simple as possible, but not simpler."
Your professional career should be as complex as it needs - but no more.
In the beginning the simpler your strategies the better.

But you'd be surprised how many artists fall victim to planning traps.
They think implementing complex, detailed strategies, they move to success.
They think that a successful career needs to be a more intricate one.
Quite simply, more moving parts do not automatically make a career better.
Add more and more complexity to make accomplishing goals harder.
Or more time-consuming, and more resource-draining.

What do we think if we see an immensely profitable, well-run business?
We automatically think it can only work that way as it's incredibly complex.
Like a magic trick it doesn't have to be and it shouldn't be.
When considering a strategy the key is to start out as simple as possible.
Is the easiest, fastest, cheapest, simplest way to know a project will buy?
There is a danger if you try to over-complicate your career.
You're in danger of costing time, money, opportunity, frustration and more.

The key to success is speed.
Complexity is the mortal enemy of speed.
Fall in love with the complex and spend more time learning than earning.
Building knowledge instead of your business.
Analyzing instead of taking action and that means more work.

Complexity always adds to your bottom line costs.
More hours spent strategizing and developing, but less progress to your goal.
No matter how much efficiency you think it may add.
No matter how much you may think it saves you.

The more complexity in a career the more sluggishly things get done.
If you work on your own, you can usually get things done relatively quickly.
Each time you say "yes" to a layer of career complexity you sacrifice speed.

The bottom line to building a successful career is all about speed.
Complexity kills speed.
Are you more likely to add more steps or options or to strip something out?
Most people will answer "add" to that question.
That's because it's far easier to add than it is to take away.

More complex does not mean better.
But what more complex does mean is more demanding.
The more resources it will require to run efficiently and effectively.
The idea is to simplify your business objectives.
Not to create the "perfectly run business" by adding to them.
Complexity your progress, and progress is more important than perfection.

What's the minimum you can give to your career?
Re-target your focus on the main goals for your career.
You'll see a vast improvement in your career no matter what level.
You'll be more productive and have more time to work on your career.
Costs go down as you eliminate unnecessary actions previously supported.

Many artists think a gallery exhibition the start of a professional career!
Artists think it's time to approach a gallery as they're ready for an exhibition.
Galleries exist to make money for its proprietor **AND** artists who exhibit there.
Holding exhibitions is one way this is done.
Galleries are not in business to provide artists with exhibition space.
Particularly if they feel like having an exhibition just to show their work!
Yet this is what most artists' seem to think they exist for!

But make sure you really are ready for this step.
Your work should be as good as the best in the gallery you hope to show in.
Anything less and you could struggle.
Commence exhibiting prematurely and after that play a catch-up game.
Chances are you won't catch up for gallery visitors have long memories.
Their first impressions of your work will be the ones that are strongest.
Those memories stay with them, no matter what you do, even years later.

You'll now realize a professional artist doesn't just produce paintings.
You also do all the tasks other small business people perform.
The amateur artist doesn't need to do these things, a professional must.
You could be frightened at the amount of money you will have to earn.
Each and every year you are in business.
If this doesn't put you off, there's a good chance you'll make.

2. What you really need to do now is prepare a career plan.

Do you know how to generate enough to pay a framer, expand and live?
A career plan provides some sort of answer but in the beginning it's a guess.
So talk to your accountant and you'll also need a lawyer/ solicitor.
It's best to select advisors who're experienced in helping people in business.
If they've assisted people in the art industry, great but they'll be hard to find.
Cheapest is not best so use accountants and solicitors sensibly to get value.

Another group of advisers will be those already in the art industry.
Other artists and galleries will provide advice, particularly on getting started.
They'll be less keen to help you become rivals though.
Don't accept it all as 'gospel' for many myths are perpetuated this way.

You may need to borrow money.
Lenders will expect to see a business plan.
The plan will help you decide how much capital you need to start with.
It's better to be pessimistic.
Your lending institution will not be impressed if you return shortly for more.
Things often go wrong in business, so you need extra to allow for this.
This is more likely to happen in the art business than most!

It is very rare for money to come rolling in, in our industry.
Your career plan is a measure against which you can judge performance.
It can be modified later, in light of your results.
It's very important you understand the main financial details.
People ask questions based on your career plan expecting you to know.
You **MUST** be involved in its preparation to have this understanding.
Your career plan will suit your particular aspirations.

But most plans have some common elements.
Artists need an income statement, balance sheet and cash flow forecast.
Estimate figures for sales, costs of sales, administration and marketing.
At the beginning this is hard.
The amounts become more accurate each time your career plan is revised.
Which means you'll need to regularly revise your business plan.
Eventually it becomes more accurate and useful as a predictor.
So you should be pessimistic at this stage for realism comes later.

You, or your accountant, must make assumptions.
They include items like the expected level of inflation and rate of taxation.
Also trends for interest rates, need for capital expenditure and its timing.
Stock turnover, time to collect money, and time to pay others are considered.

Do not be at all optimistic in preparing your career plan.
Sales frequently are slower than expected and costs are always higher!
It's better to be conservative and real life better as often it is the other way.

There's the possibility of seasonal fluctuation too.
When I had a gallery January and February were always tough months.
It could be different elsewhere, say in a popular tourist destination.
If you've lived in a place long enough, you'll have an idea of seasonal factors.
But ask other business people too.

Keep costs to an absolute minimum.
Do you really need to build a studio, or would it just be nice?
Are you having stationery printed or could you do it on your computer?
You may need to register a business name, employ an accountant etc.

Make projections for the next three years.
First monthly projections, the second quarterly and third annual forecast.
These are cash flow forecast, balance sheet and income statements.
This not only shows whether your art business is likely to be viable.
It also provides a check on the accuracy of your arithmetic.
The balance sheet shows if sufficient assets for security back cash needs.

Write down exactly what you're going to do.
Write notes on your background and past performance.
How will you market your work, the competition, your studio, and pricing?
You did your financial projections, assessment of risk, with your accountant.
Now you are close to having a business plan.
This might be helpful when you seek finance.
But importantly it will help you clarify your thinking particularly if kept concise.

But remember the idea is to simplify your business objectives.
Not to create the "perfectly run business" by adding to them.
Complexity slows progress, and progress is more important than perfection.
What's the minimum you need for your career to grow?
You might need to consider setting up your art business part time.
Until it generates sufficient income.

3. Nothing happens unless you do something.

To see ANY results you have to take ACTION.
Once you know what you need to take action on, it's much easier to actually DO it.
BUT it's **CRITICAL** you **NARROW** your focus.

Decide on three main goals you want to achieve with your art career.
Find 3 key areas to take action immediately with your professional career.
If you're just getting started your critical areas might be:
Learning how to use your time effectively.
Understanding how to write work faster AND better!
Maybe you've already mastered those areas.
BUT you're just not getting the prospects you need to really build your sales.
Then build a website, with prospect generation as the focus.

If you're well established, but want career ideas start a referral program.
Narrow your focus and you'll have a much clearer idea what you need to do.
You don't have to do everything all at once … or ever!
Implementing one or two most basic strategies can bring amazing results.

Experiment with different prices for work to see what gives most profit?
This is easier to do with prints (they could even be photo-copies).
You can then translate what you learn to marketing your original works.
Focus on implementing only a few strategies at a time and taking **ACTION**.
Keep a record of your action plans and how they turn out?

An action plan is different from a plan.
A plan is just a map which shows elements of what you want to achieve.
An action plan also has steps that lets you put the elements together.

Outline a starting point:
Take time to honestly evaluate your current situation, as well as your skills.
Decide which areas need improving but in some areas ignore improvement.
Consider just how you will improve those areas where it is needed.
List of everything you want to accomplish and put them into a priority order.
The most important and urgent are placed first.
Then the most important, followed by urgent and everything else after that.
Work out just what you want to do.
Decide how you'll deal with setbacks:
Dealing with reverses is never easy, but they are inevitable.
If you are prepared, then they become manageable at least.

Set milestones:
Break down your overall plan into smaller sections.
Set target dates for when each of the sections will be reached and passed.
As each small goal is reached, reward yourself and continue to the objective.
Adjust the plan to the most important changes according to new perspective.
Jot down some notes about your present career as an artist.
Your future success is related to the level of planning being implemented.
You should accomplish specific, tangible tasks (no matter how small) daily.
Your tasks should be defined and given a relevant time frame to complete.

Obstacles to planning:
Lack of time as daily activities are more pressing and urgent than planning.
Lack confidence plan developed gives enough improvement to justify effort.
If your business plan is in the filing cabinet, your art career is there too.
Often an external point of view can be objective and thus helpful.
Look for someone a success in business over a period of time (5+ years).
They have a genuine interest in the success of your career.
Essential starting point is why you are in business as a professional artist.
Your answer is exactly what you are about and how success is determined.
What are the natural divisions of your career?
This might be planning, finance, painting, framing, or whatever.

They are the core functions of your professional career.
Deal with each as a separate but more manageable component of the whole.
The remaining questions are asked of each component of your business.
What must we do to make this component complete?
List all that has to happen consistently for perfect result in each core function.
If the job needs to be done, then write it down.

What are the best ways to measure your performance?
How can you improve even your current best?
Something you'd like to do and can't, write down what's stopping you.
Then aim for that, an idea that needs fixing and to measure improvement.

What do you actually have to do to make each task give a best result?
List steps to reach a destination and test each so there's a clear job done.
Look at each task and identify who should perform it.
The most urgent steps generally have most impact on the bottom line.
Give all tasks a priority ranking and deal with the most important ones first.

What's the deadline?
Ask any person who is necessary, what time they need to do what's required.
Consider each step relative to cost and make sure expenditure is in budget.

3. PLANNING LEADS TO SUCCESS!
Reviewed by Bob Linger – (Bundaberg, Australia)

1. Can you survive tough times?
2. A woman became extremely successful.
3. There are two magic powers:
4. What's stopping you?
5. Is there a magic bullet?
6. How far do you need to go?

1. Can you survive tough times?

Times have been tough for many artists lately.
So what can you do?
Will you need more outlets than you've had in the past?
The answer should be a resounding yes.

So in tough times you almost certainly will need to do more works.
An outlet still needs sufficient to attract and maintain clients for your works.
Can they replace sold works?
AND freshen up your part of their display from time to time?
Multiply this by your outlets.
Now you have an idea of the number of works you will need to do.

You should move UP-market!
The further you can move up-market, the fewer paintings you'll need to sell.
Your income is then more assured.
But you must only put on sale your best work.
People will not buy unless they think your work is good value.

Don't do things now that will make it difficult down the track.
For example moving up-market doesn't necessarily mean large works.
It really means raising your prices so paint better rather than bigger.
This allows you to spend less time painting than if large works are produced.

Could you reduce your costs?
This is easier said than done.
For everyone else is trying to lift their charges which impacts on you.
Framing can reduce costs without reducing the appearance of your works.

But the main one is to paint in standard sizes.
Then you swap paintings around.
Then you don't tie up a lot of money in a frame for each work.

Take care of frames for damage costs money to repair or replace.
Also they don't do justice to your work, and may even be a barrier to sales.
Don't reduce quality, just cost as appearance is more important than ever.
Standardized works mean standardized packing, easier as well as cheaper.

Charges can be examined.
It's reasonable to be charged for sales, for sales are what you want.
60% commission if works are sold is better than 25% where they are not.
Entry fees, paid whether or not a sale, should be related to sales probability.
Implement changes gradually and then you can control them.
AND keep the **RIGHT** outlets.

2. A woman became extremely successful.

She was an African American born in Louisiana on a farm in 1865.
Her parents were former slaves but she was an orphan at age seven.
At 14, she married to escape abuse suffered from her brother-in-law.
She became a mother at 17 and a widow at 20.
Supported herself and daughter picking cotton, laundress, in barber shop.
From what I can tell, the most she ever made then was $1.50 a day.
At 25 she began to develop a condition that caused her to start balding.
Can you imagine?
As if she didn't have enough to deal with, now her hair was falling out.

But from there things improved.
She quickly became a student of "how to fix this balding problem".
In fact, she researched all kinds of treatments.
She discovered sulfur cured a scalp disease causing people to lose hair.
People lost their hair a lot back then (because they didn't bathe sufficiently).
They would get some nasty scalp infection and their hair would fall out.
But if you treated the problem with sulfur, the problem could be cured.

So she did the only logical thing to do, start her own business.
She sold a product called "Madam Walker's Wonderful Hair Grower".
She was just starting out and didn't have a big budget (probably **NO** budget).
She had no choice but to go door to door, selling her product.

Nobody really embraces a door to door sales person with open arms!
But imagine what it must have been like for Madam Walker?
It was a racist and male dominated environment back then.
How many times do you think she was rejected?
How many doors do you think were slammed in her face?
How many insults did she hear?
Mrs. Walker hung in there and sold more products, and developed new ones.
Not only did she survive …she thrived and opened a factory in Indianapolis.
By 1913, she travelled the world training women to sell her products.
She died in 1919 at age 51.
By then she had become the world's first female self-made millionaire!
Against incredible odds, wouldn't you say?

Her success was largely due to one critical characteristic:
The ability to get up and get to **WORK**.
Seems we have a lack of that ability these days.
The real secret to success is to get out there and work.
As Madam C.J. Walker shows there's absolutely **NO** excuse for failure

In the beginning, failure is pretty much inevitable.
But you have to get up, brush yourself off, and get back in the game
A plan provides the ability to get started and keep going.
It doesn't really matter if it isn't the very best plan that could be devised.
All it has to be is enough to let us get under way (like Madame Walker).
The plan can be improved as we go.

3. There are two magic powers:

Magic Power #1: The ability to get started.
Madame Walker had this magic power!
The biggest thing plaguing people struggling is the inability to get started.

Time on research, preparation and making sure all is "perfect" means:
You are scared it's not going to work.
You are frightened you're going to look stupid.
You think you might lose some money.
And you don't want to be judged.

All that stuff is almost GUARANTEED to happen!
Your very first website will probably look terrible – just look at mine!
Your friends will almost certainly judge you and talk behind your back.
They'll say what a fool you are for trying to make money as an artist.

Most will think you should get a real job.
But since you know that's all going to happen, stop worrying about it.
Better to go on ahead and power through it.
Hurry up so you can get to the good stuff.
Now you can practice Magic Power #2.

Magic Power #2: The ability to step back into the ring
An artist's career is like boxing for you will get knocked around a little.

Someone who wants to become a boxer has this conversation:
Boxer: "Coach? Can I talk to you a minute?"
Coach: "Sure, son. What's on your mind?"
Boxer: "Well, I think I want to be a boxer."
Coach: "That's great. We can start training on Monday."
Boxer: "OK. But …Coach?"
Coach: "Yeah?"
Boxer: "Do you think I'll ever get …you know …hit?"
Boxer: "Like, do you think anyone is going to …you know, punch me?"
Coach: "GET THE HELL OUT OF MY GYM!"

It never happens - in BOXING.
But it does happen in business **AND** it definitely happens in the art business.
People start (a huge feat anyway) and then get floored by the first setback.
It takes them by complete surprise and it makes them want to quit.
I suppose it's natural.
What really leads to success is an ability to brush yourself off and start over.

Like the champion boxer, you get up and step back into the ring.
If you do that enough times, you'll be tough as a pit bull and start winning.
And it doesn't take too many wins before it all starts to add up.
But if you don't get back in there and take another shot …you'll never win.
EVERYONE who achieved lasting success has, lost all before they "made it".
Often on more than one occasion.

Failure is embarrassing and sometimes scary.
Getting back up and stepping into the ring again is hard but worth it!
And if an orphaned daughter of former slaves can work her way up.
Through the racist hardship of the economically depressed deep south.
And become the world's first self-made female millionaire
What possible excuse do you have?
Do you think it was easy for her to walk outside and start going door to door?
Was it was easy to keep going after hearing insults and rejections every day?
But she did it anyway because that's what it takes sometimes.

A plan provides the ability to get started.
It doesn't really matter if it isn't the very best plan that could be devised.
All it has to be is enough to let you get under way (like Madame Walker).
Remember the plan can be improved as you go.

4. What's stopping you?

If you keep doing the same as you always do, you'll get the same result.
Well actually you'll get even worse results.
Particularly if the results haven't been as good as you'd hoped they'd be!
So there is certainly some aspect of your career you should want to change.
Maybe it's something major, or a little thing or even a number of small things.
You probably want to have success some other artists seem to have.
A sell-out exhibition instead of a few even though everyone likes the work.
Maybe you just want to catch some breath and find more stuff to paint?

Well nothing is going to happen until you do something.
You must act.
Thinking and dreaming gets nothing done even if key to deciding what to do.
The toughest part is deciding what to do **FIRST** you know what to do there.

It doesn't actually matter what you do, just so long as it is something.
Many people just waste time trying to work out the best thing to do.
Instead of starting and then turning that into the best thing you can.
Then procrastination becomes a thing of the past as well!

It is actually better to do something even without goals.
Than just spend time deciding on goals and not actually doing anything.
It doesn't matter if you are busy, disorganized, or what your excuse is.
You can fix wrong changes but if nothing happens then no change is made.
It's the status quo.

When you try to make major changes it's easy to get overwhelmed.
It's easy to become discouraged and give up.
That's definitely much easier than sticking out the tough road ahead.
You revert to old easy ways and blame yourself for your failure.
It doesn't have to be like that.
If you take things one step at a time then other habits start to develop.

Even the busiest person can find the time to take a single step.
That's all it takes to get started so you don't feel overwhelmed.
You make gradual lasting changes to your life and career.
So choose a goal that you'd like to have happen in 30 days.
Take one step at a time and generate momentum to achieving that goal.

What when you achieve it, will make a real difference to your career?
From now on it's your drive and determination to reach that goal that counts.
OK you have a goal that excites (frightens you) and you will make it happen.

What will your first step be?
This doesn't have to be major, just a step from the past towards your goal.
Do not try to make drastic changes, but **DO SOMETHING!**
It's the most important single step you take to consistently move to your goal
Even doing what seems easiest might be a good way to start!

A meaningful reason keeps you going as things get tough (they will).
Write down a list of reasons why you want to achieve this goal.
What specific benefits will you gain?
Also write down what it will cost.
This doesn't just mean money but also your emotions.
How will you feel if you do not achieve your goal?
What about when you do?

It's our emotions that drive our behaviour.
Condition your mind to drive your behaviour in ways not obviously possible.
Focus is what turns light into a laser.
The same happens if there's an emotional component to what you do!

Progress is the name of the game.
You are **NOT** aiming at perfection, just progress along the path to your goal.
Each step takes you a little closer.

There will always be setbacks and failures.
They are normal and something to be learned from.
Sometimes there may be of the two steps forward and one step back.
But you will keep progressing if you continue to take one step at a time.
It's just like doing a painting really!

5. Is there a magic bullet?

You can't become a successful money-making business overnight.
But you can hope can't you?
If contemplating a professional career, or have just begun, it is frightening.
There is often pressure from family members to get a "real job".
And you don't want to risk the family jewels chasing your dream anyway!
There **IS** an easy way to a money-making career without breaking the bank.
But you've got to do things!
You'll learn a great deal from the wrong ways, including why they're wrong.

You've also got to be patient!
Even if you do things right, you can't do them all concurrently.
That means there is no short cut for success is related to time.

Time has an effect on whatever we do.
If we have learned something we can build in ways not previously possible.
But we have to start with that initial learning.
Then relatively small ideas can become altered and improved.
That's when the context changes or they are associated with other ideas.

Most people have heard of the downward spiral or vicious circle.
Here negative momentum is the driving force.
The poor get poorer, have more children, lose jobs or can't even get a job.
Everything seems to continually get worse.

On the other hand there is an upward spiral too.
It start small and insignificantly but gradually build increased momentum.
They link with an increasing number of other ideas.
Ideas can thus spiral upwards, so that they almost seem to be self-sufficient.
Upwards spirals are integral in creative process and momentum to success.

There is no short cut but it's a spiral which you can climb aboard.
That happens if you focus on maintaining momentum rather than to the end.
It's more important to be ever more successful than to achieve success.
Even with small steps the former attitude will lead to the latter attainment.

Spirals can be powerful.
They seem to fuel themselves and become self-propelling in time.
Successful people get more opportunities to be even more successful.
Those who need opportunities never seem to get one!
Many people think this is luck, either good or bad depending on its nature.

But we make our own luck.
Good ideas can come from anywhere.
It's up to you to notice and be open to them.
You also need to harness them to your advantage.
They can be painting ideas, but career ideas are subject to the same force.

This momentum can accompany a career as it is rejuvenated.
Change will build slowly at first but gradually gain momentum.
Other spirals interlock and momentum gathers more rapidly.
In time success is attained once more.
But there is no short cut.
But some planning will steer the career.
Otherwise you are just drifting.

6. How far do you need to go?

Review the resources you have available.
Study your own information, such as your client accounts.
What is your overhead?
How long does it take to finish a typical work (say a 16" x 20" painting)?
Talk to people – often other artists are a great resource for information.

You now have too much information so sort and organize your data.
Figure out what is important in relation to your planned career.

Research should be on-going part of your daily activities.
Jot ideas down throughout the day.
Do you find you get a lot of great ideas as you're driving somewhere?
BUT you have no way to write the idea down.
Call your answering machine or mobile phone and leave a message?
Decide what needs to be done to implement the changes you are thinking of.

Keep solutions as simple as possible.
The most important thing is that your results should be easy to implement.
They should also make the changes you want.

The archer hitteth the target partly by pulling and partly by letting go.
The target is an analogy for your plan.
Letting go your baby is not an easy thing to do, particularly at first.
BUT that's what you may need to do.

You can't truly use other people's time unless you can let go.
Transition to a professional career is eased if a team manages your plan.
Most artists must be ready to make changes for this to happen.
Most of us are bits of loners as far as our art career is concerned.

Having an outside influence can be the key to ongoing prosperity.
You may wonder whether this is even possible.
BUT it's really not much different from reading what I write.
If you find something that seems to be worth a try, then you do it.
Similarly helpers whose advice and assistance is personal and immediate.

Develop a management structure that involves people other than you.
Then they can even continue when you are painting in that studio in the sky.
Your management team must know it is ability not blood that matters.
They will feel safe and become committed to your career and its prosperity.
So ask for and accept outside advice from proven competent advisors.

An outsider will certainly have skills that you need and are lacking.
Possibilities are accounting, marketing, legal or whatever a person brings.
They will see things that you don't!

Appoint a business advisor a person with business ability you respect.
BUT not your accountant or lawyer, who already have roles.
Someone from outside your immediate family with a business background.
Unbiased, objective, independent opinion won't bring excess baggage.
Have job specifications and a salary structure for everyone.
Specific job descriptions for all include yourself and family members involved.

Make sure you use the best person for any job.
Be a cheapskate and they leave so pay for performance at the market rate.
People get a feeling of self-worth rather than just doing this and a bit of that!
Their rewards are not ad-hoc BUT salaries and dividends are quite different.

Decide entry and exit criteria.
Ground rules, induction and exit program on what's best for your career.
These rules should apply to family members as well as outside advisors.
They should **NOT** be based on your relationship with individuals.
Everyone in your business gets a fair and impartial go.

Distribute information and communicate.
An artist is traditionally very secretive about his/her business.
Make sure that your career vision is communicated to everyone connected.
Well what do you need to do - get started **NOW**!
It seems like yesterday when we were all thinking about the next millennium.
It's symbolic as we thought about the future, and changes that might happen.
The time comes to stop thinking about the future and start doing something.
There are a few basic things that you can do if you want a new career future.
You may already be doing some of these, or you may want to try some out.
Either way, think about what you want from your art career.

There's no point in spending years developing the perfect career.
Work to get your idea off the ground and out the door.
Microsoft does not wait for perfection to roll out their latest product.
That is why we all need to upgrade your Microsoft software every few years!
They improve their products in the market place and you should too!

We can manage change in the following way:
Define the problem and assemble the information to deal with the problem
Map out a strategy to do something that deals with problem and implement it.
Evaluate your results and improve your plan.

4. PLAN YOUR FUTURE.
Reviewed by Pamela Griffith – (Sydney, Australia)
1. Do you need to overcome perfectionist tendencies?
2. How does professionalism link to success?
3. Can you make your dreams come true?
4. What sort of artworks sell?
5. Are you status conscious?
6. Are quality and price linked?
7. Seeking opportunity.

1. Do you need to overcome perfectionist tendencies?

Perfectionism is extolled by some as a virtue, but not me.
Strive to improve what you do by all means.
To strive for perfection aims at the impossible and inevitable disappointment.

What can you do if you have those perfectionist impulses?
Take a limited time to complete a given task and then **STICK** to those limits!
It's a good way to head off the wasted hours working on trivial things.
This will keep you from burning up an entire day.

You are the only person who expects you to have all the answers!
Take advice and direction from people who have already figured it out.
Save major chunks of time when you build on other people's experience.
Failure is a learning experience, it is inevitable some things just won't work!
Look at failure as the perfect opportunity to understand your market better.
Evaluate why it didn't work for a better understanding of client and prospect.

A perfectionist easily focuses on not having yet achieved some goals.
It can link to fear of failure so don't take a negative view of what's not done.
Take time to look at small things you accomplished and work to longer goals.
A perfectionist approach can work if you can evaluate what you are good at.
Then work at what constitutes their style.

Be realistic about what you can achieve.
Many perfectionists set themselves impossible deadlines.
They take on tasks they can't reasonably hope to complete on their own.
Then, when they inevitably fail, become depressed and self-blaming.
The result is they procrastinate more, or are obsessive with the next task.

Take a long, hard look at what you want to do in any given day.
Ask yourself if your goal is reasonable and realistic.
Is it something somebody else would be able to accomplish?
If not break the goal into smaller chunks.

Focus on completing a small piece at a time.
Remember that it's not just the end goal that matters.
The smaller milestones you complete along the way are successes too.
Recognize that you are your biggest critic.
Good enough is best for stable, successful, healthy, happy career!

2. How does professionalism link to success?

Is professionalism related to success?
It does seem as if success and professionalism are related.
Success is in achieving the goals you set.
Success may be economic, creative, or whatever other goals you choose.
To be successful you must achieve the goals, or at least move towards them.
If you have no goals you can't be successful.

Professionalism is in the way you go about achieving those goals.
It's about whether you actually set goals in the first place.
Also how you check your progress towards realizing your ambitions.
It's planning, making the best of circumstances, and giving the best shot.
It's not about compromise, unless it moves you toward predetermined goals.

Professionalism is an attitude towards what you're doing.
Professionalism is only economic if your goals are too.
It's the difference, between successful artists and those who want to be.
A professional artist is careful about client perception of value of their works.
It's a perception that is very fragile and easily damaged.
Each is like a porcelain tea set, if a piece is damaged; all are lesser in value.
I'm not talking about actual physical damage but perceived value damage.
Constantly be on your guard; to maintain a high value perception.
A poor work can reduce value of all if the perception is changed sufficiently.

But it is also important to avoid actual damage to your works.
How a gallery you consider stacks artworks when are out of public view?
Are they stacked face to face and back to back?
That way the works and their frames are least likely to be damaged.
Insist white cotton gloves be worn at all galleries handling your works,
All public gallery employees wear white cotton gloves when handling works.
Why not commercial galleries too, and even (more so) art show organizers?

This tells the gallery people you value your works and they should too.
This message is also conveyed to their (and your) clients.
OK that's one way you can convey an appreciation of value for your works.
They warrant museum like handling, and they're precious.
Follow through with the white gloves by giving them a pair.

Now what about if one of your galleries doesn't do this?
No problem if 1000's of miles / kilometres from the nearest other outlet.
What if they're closer, a few hundred miles, different suburb in the same city?
Still no problem you might say!

What if one of your clients visits several galleries, as many do?
They come across one not handling your work in the appropriate manner.
What do they think?
Well at least they'll think that gallery is a lesser gallery, as indeed it may be.
They think you don't enforce your own standard or aren't aware of a breach!
It's also likely they'll wonder why you have works here at all.

This can start to erode confidence in the value of your works.
Many leading artists will not show works in what they deem lesser outlets.
It's not just few fewer sales, but to preserve the perceived value of all works.
Having works for sale in lesser outlets will reduces value in better ones.
If clients are aware of this although this could increase value in lesser outlets!
Some better galleries insist you not show in lesser outlets to preserve value!

Where would you rather sell at, a better outlet or a lesser one?
A lesser outlet can be very good for selling lesser works (if you do them).
Also for selling works hard to move elsewhere (reduce price considerably).
They're a wholesale outlet with focus on turning stock to recover something.
Instead of obtaining the best price for the best works.
You can use auctions this way too.
They are these days a big part of the selling process.

However, even this strategy needs to be handled carefully.
Some better galleries will object to this as well!
In the end the best outlets are valuable and worth keeping.

3. Can you make your dreams come true?

Dreams will NOT come true unless you believe they can.
Even lottery winners have to believe, or they wouldn't buy tickets.
We're all working at making our dreams come true.
How can we turn this into reality and become successful?

Dreams are the foundation for beliefs.
The key to happiness is having dreams.
The key to success is making your dreams come true.
Full time artists, working at making dreams come true, show it's possible.
There are also many who would like to be.
These people have a dream and they want to make it come true.
They provide inspiration for dreams being reality by keeping the dream alive.
Having your work in a gallery might be an important part of a dream.
Understanding how to go about it will certainly make the journey easier.
But it's not easy, for you actually have to do it.

What do you think you need to accomplish before you are successful?
Being rich and famous?
Gaining government support,
Having interest from art museums,
Having regular exhibitions in big city galleries,
Having sell out exhibitions,
Being a celebrity,
Having articles in newspapers or art magazines or appearing on TV
Being selected for Art fairs and juried shows,
Having a listing in an art who's who?

Many artists definition of success is linked to income from sales.
In my view, they are professional artists.
But face the facts: your prices will fluctuate!
The price of your art has very little to do with what it looks like.
It is about what the market will bear, supply and demand, and sales history.
In deciding a price for a work, look at price people will to pay for **YOUR** work.
That is how you establish a market value.

You will not get discovered or rediscovered either.
Marketing your art is hard and constant work so stop making excuses.
BEFORE success happens you must **ACT** to do the hard work it takes.
There must be regular time set aside to do business stuff.
This is **NOT** an option – it is essential for a professional artist.

Your records should be impeccable.
You never know when you might need to argue with a gallery.
Possibly works have been stolen or just lost or even damaged.

Provide detailed information on works people donate to a museum.
In addition people will inherit works and require information and validation.
Some divorce cases could also need this information.
You can even charge for a validation and certificate!

If you have a retrospective exhibition YOU need this information.
If you don't know the owner then you can't borrow it back can you?
You might need photographs too!

Pamela Griffith has records of price lists, catalogues and invitations.
She tracks where and when a work was sold and follow movement over time.
She even has a record detailing an etching of the Old Brewery Gallery.
That was my gallery from thirty years ago!

Thousands of artists make extraordinary efforts to promote their work.
You should be one of them.
They might use Facebook, Instagram or Twitter.
There certainly needs to be publicity leading up to any exhibition.
You won't find a gallery understands your work and passionate about it.
Many galleries are passionate about artists they represent and are articulate.
But the majority, are primarily interested in selling artworks.

This is not necessarily a bad thing, if making sales is a major goal.
Stop dreaming of the one person out there who can be your "art soul mate".
Galleries are in business to sell artworks and is what you expect them to do.
They do not need to understand your work, nor be emotionally moved by it.
They have contacts and collectors who like your work and want to buy.
But there are exceptions like Vollard and Picasso.
Although it might be a case of the exception proves the rule?

Let's assume you want to live above the poverty level.
You might still find it difficult to make a living from the sale of your work.
In most countries to make a living you need to sell $150,000+ of your works.
That might provide $75,000 before tax or a net income of about $50,000.
Deduct expenses, studio, art supplies, framing, advertising or promotion.
That is an ordinary income!

In recent years many previously successful artists don't get that much.
Some people even think the successful artist is actually a myth.

It certainly has been promoted that way.
Calculate how many paintings you need to sell a year, at your usual price.
Now you'll have an idea whether it is possible to earn the above income.
If you can't, then at least you have an understanding of the task ahead.

BUT it is possible although it will take time and persistence.
Wait for it to happen without accepting the odds and do yourself a disservice.
If you do the math and determine you might make a living but it isn't easy!
Maintaining a career perspective is a key to being a professional.
Every day is about career development.
Every day you continue to build your career.

A career is a network of components all contribute to an overall results.
The key to a successful career is **NOT** what you sell but **HOW** you sell!
Get the whole picture and you understand the parts (even those missing).
Your career provides an integrated vision.
It's a system for producing works for clients which result in profit for you.
Your development as an artist and making money look after themselves.
Your career aim is to find and keep clients - profitably.

Pamela Griffith – Sydney, Australia has had clients for a lifetime.
But often they eventually want to downsize and want to sell.
So they contact her (and you too) for information.
Pamela tells them to send the work to an auction if she thinks it has appeal.
She will also put them on to a gallery where there is a demand for her work.
She cautions on how long it may take to find a buyer.
She can say what price the work should achieve at auction or private gallery.

Market forces change so she suggests to keep work for the right time.
If she is having a major exhibition with a lot of publicity is a good time.
A seller could piggy-back that at an auction, or on eBay or a nearby gallery.
Otherwise they should keep it for their children.
Another alternative she suggests is to use it for a wedding present.

Investing in your work is like joining an exclusive club for a prospect.
Limit buying opportunities at first so people are keen and buying is urgent.
Take your time, be respectful make people feel important and give attention.
The work/sale is a mirror of yourself but many artists prefer not to sell/
They distance themselves from buyers to preserve a sincere artist image.
They get someone else (wife/husband) to step in to make the actual sale.
But it is really a specialist job for a gallery or agent.

Do you have a dream of what will it be like when you are successful?
How will you act then, start acting now like an already a successful artist!
Act like you are building the career that you want right from the start.
Every day is about career development so every day you build your career.
Often an artist's definition of success is linked to income generated by sales.
In my view, they are professional artists.

4. What sort of artworks sell?

It's obvious there should be answers to this question.
Otherwise neither you nor the gallery will be sure of directions to head.
But even people who ask this question know it's not easy.
That's the kind of question asked, and answered, in other areas of business.

Big business spends money to find out and predict years ahead.
What sort of cars are people buying, what TV programs do people watch?
They want answers for they know rewards are great if the answer is right.

It's even done in non-business circles.
Political parties are big poll users, surveying what people want, how they act.
There's little research in the art area, but there are ways to do it for yourself.
Want to find out what subject is popular, ask a seller of reproduction prints?
This may be your picture framer.
Reproduction prints are in just about every subject that you can think of.
And many more than you could possibly do.
If a framer says florals are selling well you know this subject has many fans.

But it also means florals are popular with this framer's clients
Perhaps this is mainly what is offered?
In most cases people are buying reproduction prints not original paintings.
There may be differences because of this.
No matter it's a start in market research for you have something to go on.
If floral paintings interest you, then test in a small way.
If the result of your test is favorable you can embark on a larger project.

Work you have passion and commitment for is likely what you do best.
Hold that vision and it'll be what you sell best, particularly in the long term.
You have an intense interest in ecology and regularly go to wilderness areas.
The subject will naturally interest you and you'll capture it how others don't.
More importantly you'll be committed to keep going long enough to do it well.
Eventually you'll become known for your wilderness paintings.
To be well known requires many people are aware of what you do.
This takes time and commitment to stay long enough for it to happen.

Think about van Gogh, Monet, Picasso, and other well-known artists.
You'll understand that once a reputation is established it works for you.
It takes a long time to grow reputation so don't abandon it lightly or too soon.

Now it's also true to say galleries basically sell what galleries promote.
With enthusiasm and intelligent effort to sell anything, it can be done.

It's not necessarily easy though.
Is your gallery director is literate and can write about you and your career?
They need sufficient capital to advertise your work to build your career.

Galleries sell what buyers are familiar with which s not quite the same.
Although with promotion of the sort implied, your works can become familiar.
This is the **REAL ANSWER** to the question about what sells.

Familiarity is the key to selling!
Particular artists and subjects benefit according to promotion or familiarity.
To promote you a gallery director may take you and a client out occasionally.
But you need to know how to behave and even how to dress.
Otherwise potential sales could evaporate.

A gallery stocks an increasing number of rain forest paintings.
There's likely to be an increase in interest in this type.
This would be particularly true in North Queensland rather than where I live.
At Pamela Griffith's exhibition at the Perc Tucker Gallery, Townsville.
Two visitors' books were filled with compliments.
The gallery acquired works and will keep supporting Pamela in future shows.
Her subject was based on local material as she camped there in a caravan.
Stories were of crocodiles, wild pigs, ship wrecked sailors and aborigines.
Although sales were only for the smaller cheaper works.
Pamela thinks prices for the larger works were above local budgets.

I think having 50 works for sale may have also been a problem.
But for Pamela the exhibition was worth doing.
A great publication was produced and her prestige enhanced.
But even more importantly it lead to **TWO** other major opportunities.

The status of the artist matters, which means if you are well known.
In other words familiar to many people.
Then you can sell almost anywhere there.
In a particular gallery an artist may have status that is not as broad as this.
They're the best local artist, own the gallery or well promoted by the gallery.
They sell well there, but not in others where the familiarity factor is absent.
Not only does status have an influence over whether a sale takes place.

It will also influence the price that can be obtained.
Unknown artists, no matter how 'good', cannot obtain high prices.
Established and familiar to buyers and possible buyers reward by high price.

Are there other factors?
Subject matter and color used do influence the buying decision.
Green and blue works are difficult to sell, compared to warmer tones.
Familiar subject matter will sell more easily than the unusual.

So becoming familiar is important.
There are things you or your gallery can do to help this process along.
Personal appearances are important, so exhibitions are familiarization.

5. Are you status conscious?

Status is about social position.
A characteristic of a society is variety and nature of social position.
It's a fact we can turn to our advantage, if we are aware, and make use of it.
A basic human need is to be aware of social position.
The art business is most definitely a part of culture or society.
We need to understand how other people think and behave when they buy.
Understanding this psychology is a key to successful sales at any time.

Every time people buy, they'll seek to satisfy a basic human need.
Everyone has a perceived rank and it's normal to want to go to a higher level.
Acquiring objects, services or experiences, linked to a desired level, is how.
Whatever the object, the want being expressed is the same.
There's a need to belong to a particular social group (such as artists).
There are even people who think they do not care about social position.
BUT that's actually the group they belong to – those who don't care.
Whatever group, buying artwork is often a way to reward themselves.

How can we turn this knowledge into sales at any time?
Status symbols aren't always fixed but objects, services or experiences.
We sell objects (paintings), services (lessons), or experiences (art tours).
Link to a high status person or thing status can transfer to what we sell.
You must be consistent, but it really is that easy.
Status does rub off onto whatever is around it.

So endorsements are a powerful way to add status.
An artist photo in a US art magazine presenting a painting to the president.
The photo is a powerful builder of status as the artist is more important too.
Other clients can bask in the reflected status given by the important person.
'The President has a Joe Bloggs too, you know.'
It can be worth giving a work to a prominent person.
Provided they're photographed with it, and preferably yourself as well.
A testimonial from the prominent person adds further to the endorsement.
So endorsements are a powerful way to add status.

But you must use the photos!
Just sticking them in an album of memories does nothing for your sales.
Many people as possible should see you, your work and a famous person.
That's what being conscious of status is about!
Blogging and tweeting can be used as well for these promotions.
High status people don't have to be art collectors just linked to your art.
It's even possible they might not like your art.

That doesn't matter, provided it doesn't become public knowledge.
Although if they do not appreciate the gift they might also on-sell it.
This caution also applies to your own friends.
The famous person could be sports person, TV star, politician, or 'celebrity'.
Anyone who is well known can add status to you and your art.
All you need is the evidence and to promote the link.

Artists list people who bought their work or collections with their work.
That's just a step in the right direction.
BUT it is unsophisticated and will have little influence on most people.
Other artists, academics and curators might look at your list, but that's all!
A photograph of a work hanging in the most prestigious collection is better.
Even without the photographs, don't just list the owners.

Use the information to convey status.
But you must promote the linkage for the status to adhere to your works.
A mere listing does not do this, but selective quotes from the owners would!

There are many products that gain status through pricing.
Designer jeans, some wines, Rolex watch, Rolls Royce cars, are examples.
Original artwork is perceived to be a status product, so we're there too.
Some artist's works have more status and are considerably more expensive.
So how can you move up the status ladder?

One approach is to put your prices up, even considerably.
Also spend a great deal on superb frames.
Then justify the higher price in terms of status.
Don't forget those famous people photographed with one of your works.
No-one has to know you are related to them do they?

So now you can see why artists should be conscious of status.
An increase in status can lead to an increase in sales at higher price levels.
Don't just put prices up; make the link with higher status at the same time.

6. Are quality and price linked?

There's been research into links between wine quality and price.
Study published on 14th January 2008 by the National Academy of Sciences.
Reports on the study were usually associated with sensationalist headlines.
But a synthesis of several of them is as follows:

Higher wine prices boost drinking pleasure.
In a demonstration of the power of marketing by researchers in California.
They show you can increase a person's wine enjoyment by increasing price.

C. I. T. Professor of Economics, Antonio Rangel led the team.
They tested how marketing shapes consumers' perceptions.
And whether it also enhances their enjoyment of the product.
21 volunteers sampled 5 different bottles of Cabernet Sauvignon rating taste.
The taste test was run 15 times, with wines presented in random order.
The taste test was blind except for information on the price of the wine.
Without telling volunteers, the researchers presented two of the wines twice.
Once with the true price tag and again with a fake one.
They also passed off a $90 bottle of Cabernet Sauvignon as a $10 bottle.
And presented a $5 bottle as worth $45.

As well as collecting the test subjects' impressions of the wines.
Brains were scanned to monitor activity in the medial orbitofrontal cortex.
Quality should trigger activity in there - thought to show pleasure.
Researchers found people expect wines that cost more to be higher quality.
They believe those wines provide more pleasure than less expensive ones.
When 21 adult test subjects sampled the same wine at different prices.
They reported pleasure at significantly higher levels if told a wine cost more.
At the same time the brain area responsible for pleasure was more active.
Inflating the price of a bottle of wine enhanced drinking experience.
This was neural activity but the part of the brain interprets taste was not.

Volunteers consistently gave higher rating to more "expensive" wines.
Brain scans show neural activity in pleasure centres with expensive wine.
Indicating the increased pleasure they reported was a real effect in the brain.
The more wine costs, the more people enjoy it, regardless of how it tastes.
Many studies have looked at how marketing affects behaviour.
This is the first study to show that it has a direct effect on the brain.
We've known for a long time people's perceptions are affected by marketing.
Now we know the brain itself is modulated by price. Baba Shiv study author.
People's beliefs about quality of a wine affect how well it tastes for the brain.

If an experience is pleasurable, the brain uses it to guide future choice.
A conclusion with implications for marketing influencing quality perceptions.
Expert rating, peer review, country of origin, store and brand names.
Also repeated exposure to advertisements.
If people believe expert ratings, that should influence tasting experience.

It also has equally important implications for marketing artworks.
It is likely similar research in a range of works would produce similar results.
For example the more a work costs, people assume it is a quality work.
Regardless of what it really looks like.
Have you witnessed that actually happen?

That marketing affects behavior is self-evident.
Otherwise there is no point, marketing is **MEANT** to influence behavior!
The brain pleasure centre influenced by a tasting experience linked to price.
A similar influence where a visual experience is linked to price is probable.
It is likely price is just one factor influences the viewing or tasting experience.
The study reported, only investigated the influence of price.
The study showed the brain's reward centre considering subjective beliefs.
Other subjective factors are likely to have a similar influence.

Marketers have assumed these latest results to be true for a long time.
Prestige brands are marketed in a way that these finding support.
Generally such brands have resisted any thought of reducing price.
Those who had price reductions have found their prestige image eroded.
The reported research supports what actually happens in the marketplace.
Research makes no difference when trade on price - quality is irrelevant.

When he was alive van Gogh paintings couldn't find a buyer.
But these days they are the top of the prestige tree.
The works haven't changed, they are still the same as they've always been.
What has changed has been the perception of value of those works.
This perception of value lies in people's minds.
This has been influenced by art historians, critics and prices for his works.

Is there any such thing as good art?
What exactly is quality when applied to art works?
Is this any different from wine quality?
How does this influence the marketing of your own works?

7. Seeking opportunity.

Opportunity is everywhere.
A successful person recognises and seizes opportunity any time and place.
But you won't recognise opportunity unless you look for it.

You go looking for opportunity, rather than waiting for it to knock.
Basically all the time you should be saying to yourself, what can I do here?
How can I be part of this?
Is there something I could do?
How could these people use what I can offer?
Where do I fit in?
And so on.

In unlikely places, opportunity arises for a person open and receptive.
A barrier to opportunity's knock is know in advance opportunity's knock.
In other words a closed mind is a guarantee opportunity will not knock.
Or will not be recognised if it does.
A scientist conducting an experiment sets out to test different possibilities.
Not just the one he expects to provide the answer he seeks.
He is looking for success, the expected outcome, but open to other possibilities also.
Sometimes a break-through in science comes from unexpected outcomes.
They open up a new line of thinking.
Provide solutions to quite different problems than the one initially focused on.

You should approach success in a scientific way.
Certainly have a focus, but keep your eye out for other possibilities too.
I know an artist who has spent most of his life as a contemporary artist.
He also branched into sculpture; a move, which almost sent him broke.
The works were equivalent in standard but the money side was not.
Eventually many of the fine works were consigned to the local scrap heap!
This same artist has also illustrated children's books.
Illustrations are not like his 'artistic' works but he enjoys it and it pays well.

There's a lot more to this artist's story than I've outlined.
It illustrates a scientific attitude to his career, as distinct from what he paints.
He has kept his mind open to other possibilities and tried them out.
Even one that was quite different (illustration).
This story spans probably 20 or more years too.
He is not an art student trying something this week, next something else.

There has to be a serious exploration of the opportunities presented.
To discover what is possible both in an artistic and also a career sense.
My life lead me to believe many best opportunities come at times of disaster.
The phoenix arises from the ashes – like the cleansing power of a bushfire.
At first, waste and ruin, then green shoots poke through a blackened surface.
Life goes on, and it's the same for us.
Perhaps when faced with an impending, or actual disaster.
That's when we really need to focus on even the smallest opportunity.
An opportunity which otherwise may have gone unnoticed.

Creativity is a response to adversity.
It's no accident that many successful people did not have a great start in life.
They learnt to be creative and look for opportunity.
The tragedy is others from similar or better beginnings did not do the same.
Truly opportunities for success are everywhere; we just have to look.

Many people are blind to the opportunities that surround them.
But opportunity comes with hard work, do something to get anything!
It is likely opportunities are not often clearly sign-posted.
They don't have a sign $1 million available for doing this, like lotto signs.
You have to take the opportunity to find out what the reward is.
This is what it's like in real life, rather than that of lotto dreams.
A best opportunity can slip away without trace if there is little or no effort'
Every part of realizing an opportunity must be accompanied by your best.
Otherwise the opportunity diminishes.
Courage and persistence you **CAN** make the most of opportunities arising.

You also need to seek out opportunities.
Ask yourself questions.
Where could this lead?
What could happen next?
What if (you fill in the rest)?

You must seek out opportunity or most will just pass you by.
There's no point hoping opportunity comes your way.
You must actively seek it.

5. POTENTIAL ACTIVITY.

Reviewed by Susanna Hawkes – (Perth, Western Australia.)
1. Making major sales.
2. Many artists run their own gallery.
3. Become an artists' agent.
4. Can you make money from teaching?

1. Making major sales.

You'll need to maintain or increase the value of your works.
So you move up market.
But at the highest price levels, special sales skills are required.
Many standard selling techniques, do not work when making major sales.
There is actual research evidence to back these statements.
Fortunately you can easily learn those skills.

What is a larger sale anyway?
It's not just price although certainly that's one element.
Impact on other people is another.
For in some instances a purchase is the criteria by which people are judged.
A new car or house, are public statements about status, taste, and affluence.
By their very nature most artworks are obvious too.
Are your artworks highly priced, large, or somewhat unusual?
Then pay attention to this reality.
Just about every major sale has four steps.

Preliminary:
Activity includes introductions, starting conversation and initial impressions.
The potential client forms an impression of the sales person in this phase.
In larger sales this is not as important as for smaller sales.

Investigative:
Asking questions is basic to just about every sale of whatever kind.
You uncover needs or gain a better understanding of what a client wants.
It's the most important aspect of selling, particularly with larger sales.

Capability:
You must demonstrate you have something worthwhile.
In larger sales it's almost always a solution to a client problem.
How can your painting solve a client's problem?
You need to know what the problem is but you should do that previously.
Then you demonstrate how the painting provides an answer, or part solution.

Obtain commitment:

In small sales usually a purchase **BUT** larger ones a series of commitments.
You now get to talk to the managing director, or the husband, for example.
Traditional techniques are ineffective when making larger sales.
This is a sequence of events rather than precise steps.
It's possible to enter at anywhere, but usually the sequence is maintained.
This is a simple process and is carried out by asking questions.

You should advance to the next stage in the sequence.

It is important to keep advancing from a previous position than anything.
At each stage you should move a step closer to making a sale.
The biggest mistake is to try and jump to the end too quickly.
The client must feel comfortable all the way through the sale process.
If the sales person (you or gallery) does this, then buying is inevitable result.

2. Many artists run their own gallery.

Here's a different approach as a way of organizing a gallery.
I call this the Market oriented gallery as opposed to a Viewer oriented gallery.
What is the viewer-oriented gallery like?
The Viewer oriented gallery is organized to emphasize **VIEWING** artworks.
Care to lighting, how works hung, the focus is on works and presentation.
National, State and regional Galleries are all set up this way.
Most galleries are set up and operate using this philosophy, so yours might.

So how is this other way different?
On the other hand the Market oriented gallery is set up to **SELL** artworks.
Anything done is to help sell the works, whether on display or not.
It's like the difference between a library and a book-shop!
A possible difference could be labels attached to, or near, each work.
In a viewer-oriented gallery they are usually very informative.
Title, media, measurements, date, artist's name are usually there.
Often price and even be biographical or critical information as well.

But a market oriented gallery may have no label, or just a title.
Viewers seek information usually provided in a viewer oriented gallery.
A viewer also has to get engaged in a conversation with the sales person!
Lack of information helps a sales person identify interested potential buyers.
Too much information, potential buyers are anonymous unless they buy.
The opportunity to turn potential buyers into actual buyers is lost.

Let's say you want to make your gallery a more efficient way of selling?
Do you still do many things that are carry-over from viewer-oriented gallery?
Of course you do, but you should think things through.
For example it's quite likely, when you are open, anybody can come in.
What's wrong with that you might say?
It's an inefficient use of your time to be waiting in case someone comes in.

You should be operating by appointment instead.
This is not usual in galleries, but there are some that do.
Accountants, solicitors, hairdressers, and other professionals' value time.
You make appointments to use their services why not the same for you?

In addition, many people who visit galleries are lookers.
This is not too surprising, for that's how we enjoy art isn't it?
If they have no intention of buying, in the motor-trade they're 'tyre-kickers'.
Car salesmen don't waste time on tyre-kickers – there is no commission.
The Viewer oriented gallery is set up to attract lookers or artistic tyre-kickers.

Wouldn't it be better if only buyers, or potential buyers, came in?
As it stands you have to sort the people out, after they arrive.
You could also have a section of your gallery, open to the general public.
Then only at certain times according to your marketing plans.
In other words have people calling when you want them.

Your Market oriented gallery can focus on Exhibitions.
They represent the best chance for bulk sales for you and any other artists.
Work on display, in an accessible stock area, can be preliminary advertising.
People look at a work you tell them of a forthcoming exhibition or new print.
You provide details such as when it's on, or will be available, and so forth.
You can also ask the client if they'd like to be mailed about this.
Thus add to the number of potential buyers for your work.
The risk is a buyer decides to wait for the exhibition or print and not buy now.
This is O.K. if you don't really need the money now.
Unfortunately there's also a risk the potential client does not buy then either.
If you are in a tourist area, this is quite likely.

Then the best strategy is to try and have the client buy now.
If successful get a name and address for the exhibition, other promotion.
Then they can buy again.
If they do not buy now, but show interest capture their name and addresses.

Would the gallery layout be different?
A welcome area to have cups of tea, coffee, a drink and something to eat.
Generally a place for relaxation prior to an interview with you.

Do not depend on the work selling itself.
But if a visitor wants information and wants it now, give it to them.
For many other people you'd be better off setting up an appointment.
Then discuss what you have available and how this can meet their needs.
Buyers need assistance use literature to discuss needs and get questions.

Don't give anything even sales stuff before getting contact details.
This information opens the door to sales in the future.
Do not worry at all about people who don't show interest.
No sales from stock doesn't mean an exhibition or print will be unsuccessful.
There's no correlation between sales from stock and success of promotions.
What you write for clients is important for the written word is very powerful.
Brochures, fliers and handouts are carefully crafted for maximum effect.
There's a great deal of thought that goes into the best sales literature.

A mere CV is not sufficient.
Most go unread into the wastepaper basket, or read later when it's too late.
For a complex product, like art, literature may actually hinder purchasing.

That's why one approach is to give NO literature.
You're better talking to the people and finding out their requirements.
Than if they make an assessment from the literature.
Particularly from sales pieces sent to a prospect, like exhibition invitations.

What if a prospect can't find what they want in the written material?
They may not come and look at the actual work.
Send written material so people come to a studio, gallery or exhibition.
Have other material available or specially to follow up an initial contact.
This way you can have the right literature available for a particular job.

Creating literature just for a particular event or exhibition is worthwhile.
But, display only sample copies of this material.
Then use the prospect's interest to obtain leads for following up.
You must get visitor's details, like name and address, to contact them later.

How do you develop literature that works?
Well the more specific it is the better.
Write a flyer describing your key benefits.
Make sure these are for the people who're likely to receive the literature.
When writing your sales literature, take an aggressive approach.
Keep a potential buyer in mind, what do they want and how will they decide?
Is an individual making the decision or will it be a couple or a group?
What criteria will be important for them?

What will you use the literature for?
You may need to create different sales pieces for different sorts of prospects.
What have past clients had to say about your work?
What has been written in magazines or newspapers?

Testimonials are powerful, because they're not you saying it.
Make sure you collect them, and use them, they're a most important sale aid.
Design your literature to show the benefits and advantages for the client.
Show how your work meets their needs and avoid long winded paragraphs.
It's a good idea to provide after-sales literature.
This will be designed to help people.
Then they can talk to their friends about you and your work.
A list of common questions with suggested answers could be a start?

2. Become an artists' agent.

You'll need these qualities:
'Many of the qualities that make people successful in sport are exactly the qualities that make people successful in business and in life.' (77)
"Strong self-discipline and intelligent self-management are in my view the fundamental building blocks for all success.' (77)
'If there's self-discipline then repetitive activity is not a grind to the athlete, only to someone looking on. This self-discipline increases the fun, enjoyment and satisfaction of involvement. The grind is when people work in jobs they dislike to earn money to enjoy things they like.'
Don Talbot – Australian swimming coach, in "Nothing but the best".

A serious commitment to be an agent requires honest assessment.
What do you want to achieve by being an agent?
What do you have to do to get that?
Are you prepared to pay the price?
What are the implications as a result of your answers?
You'll also need self-management.
How do you organize your life around this commitment?
How can you conduct yourself?
Can you shape your life so that you maximize opportunities?
Can you make the money you need to keep doing it?
Commitment means living a lifestyle that will take you in the right direction.

Setting targets - don't set the bar too low.
Is a development program correct, support system in place and appropriate?
You should be able to make serious progress to whatever goals you have.
There is no need to make a public declaration as that only adds pressure.

What is an ideal agent like?
Unless you have an answer, you don't know if you want to be one or not.
AND what kind of agent you want.
The main value of an agent is they save you time **BUT** they cost money.

An ideal agent is:
Someone such as a husband, wife, best friend or similar of an artist.
They care about the artist, and their art, and want to see them successful.
They would like to help them along and share in their success.

Do you fit the above description?
Do you need the money?
It is better if you don't as it's likely to take some time to generate income.

It's also desirable that you have an accounting or legal background.
You will be negotiating and/or dealing in financial matters.
Knowledge of those professions is actually more useful than art background.
Fortunately you only need some legal or accounting to be an effective agent.
It's possible for someone to learn these things as they go.

Actors, authors, models, musicians, media, sports people have agents.
The agent and people they represent, make considerable sums of money.
Not long ago their present clients were like artists are these days.

So there's a great opportunity for such a profession to grow.
Lawyers and accountants are backgrounds from which agents are drawn.
They have expertise in negotiating, drawing up contracts, finance and so on.
They are not usually former elite sports players.
Art galleries are often agents for their artists.

BUT being an agent is NOT the same as being a travelling salesman!
The artist or artists are your employer(s).
They need to know what you are doing and will make decisions if necessary.
You will learn what to do as an agent by doing.
You'll learn by marketing and selling their work for a probationary period.
No money made for the artist = continued probationary period.
The artist learns gradually in the same way.

The more successful the artist the more they need an agent.
But then they'll want, and be able to afford, you as their agent.
And you'll do the things they do not want to do, or feel incapable of doing.
This involves more than inviting someone to their studio, or view a website.
Or to even show a portfolio accompanied by slides.

Making money is a key driver, failure to make money is out of business.
Art professionals need opportunities to make money from paintings.
If they can sell enough, or prices are high enough they might be interested.
An artist's main thrust is how they can make money by selling their art.
Solve their problem and they'll solve yours!

Most artists consider their job is to produce artworks.
Once a painting is completed it's time to get started on the next one.
The question of selling hardly arises as it is assumed it will happen.
Provided the work is of a suitable standard and in an appropriate location.

Many artists think people fall in love with their work.
They will want to sell or buy it as the case may be.

But unfortunately this rarely happens.
Working alone in isolation, they can fall in love with their own work.
They are the only person who falls in love with their own artwork regularly.
BUT they're not a buyer!

There must be a good rapport between the artist and agent.
That will allow open and frank feedback from both sides.
Credible accounting systems are essential, particularly on your part.
This will go a long way to exposing any dishonesty.
Saying work x was sold for $400 when it actually $500, shouldn't happen!
There must be an agreement about how any money earned is apportioned.
Know exactly what the financial structure is before you get involved.

You should determine your position in order to negotiate a fair fee.
Decide whether you can cope with the pricing aspect and still make a profit.
Unknown artists can't expect a high return until their work is better known.
How will adding a middleman effect sales or any return from those sales?

3. Can you make money from teaching?

You may be thinking of teaching?
It's a way to supplement your income and is very rewarding in its own right.
The best teachers enjoy it and get a satisfaction helping their students.
Then your art knowledge can become regular income?
The right qualifications you can teach in schools, colleges and universities.
What if none of these are possible **BUT** you want to teach for extra money?
That means you'll have to start your own art classes.
BUT there are advantages in doing it yourself?
You can conduct them at times to suit you.

Teach what you know best.
BUT if you want a curriculum then look at
This link is to an ebook that can help you:
> http://www.amazon.com/dp/B07KK3Y9F5

An alternative is an identical book:
> http://www.amazon.com/dp/1731347324

But it's a business you'll be running, not a hobby.

Will you receive sufficient money to make it worthwhile?
Many artists are paid poorly for teaching, because they don't ask enough.
They price based on what others charge, or wouldn't pay more themselves.
There's nothing worse than spending hours preparing and doing something.
Then not being adequately rewarded for it.

Just to illustrate what is possible.
Business people recognize the value of what they learn, better than artists.
People in business pay $100's and even $1000's for one day courses.
Often these courses are attended by hundreds of people!
Artists don't usually have the money to spend that business people might.
But people wanting to become artists might.

Just to make sure you get the idea, let's do some sums.
A one-day course attracting 250 people at $250 a head will gross $52,500!
That's a lot of money to play with.
It's possible to advertise a course well, provide meals and do a top notch job.
It's also possible to do it all again next week, somewhere else.
You don't need to run many courses like this to make very serious money.

By contrast, an artist might charge $5, for a three-hour session.
This goes for 35 weeks of the year and earns $175 per student per year.
Typically an artist starts with 10 students as they can't deal with more.

However after 10 weeks there are only five students left.
In this scenario, the artist receives around $1125.
You'd really have to love teaching or be desperate for money, wouldn't you?
Between the two extremes suggested above, there is a better way.
It may not be possible to obtain business type money, but use their thinking.
Then make better money than you otherwise might.

Ask for your money up front.
In other words people have to pay for the whole course before they start.
That's what happens at schools, and universities, and in business.
People paying up front at the start for a whole course reduces any drop off.
This is because people have made a commitment to go the distance.

Pay in advance and you don't have to collect money weekly.
You can focus on your teaching, rather than money collecting.
You have made the same commitment too.
That means now you can plan ahead and actually do some serious teaching.

People who pay weekly only have a weekly commitment.
That has to be renewed each week.
If people pay in advance means you'll receive all the money you anticipate.
You can spend a bit to make your course better if you want.
There'll probably still be some drop off to contend with.
For there's always external circumstances over which you've no control.
If you are incompetent, people will not keep coming, even if they've paid.
Eventually no-one enrolls in future courses but you don't lose money now.

Paying in advance means people have to pay more money all at once.
It may be more difficult to find $500 than $5, particularly early in the year.
Become more professional - provide credit card facilities.
People pay up front and off their credit card at what they're comfortable with.

You can offer discounts too.
For example, say you want $600 from each student.
Price your course fee at $900 and offer 1/3 off if paid before the course start.

Many people will find the money to save $300.
Perhaps you could even offer a weekly fee, but make it quite expensive.
Then it's not very attractive.
Say $35 a session so if for 35 sessions in a year, paying weekly is $1225.
Paying by credit card with early payment discount has a great deal of sense.
$600 represents less than half the price of paying weekly.

Set your courses up like this.
You'll be surprised at how few weekly paying students you'll have.

Are you paid what you are worth?
It's **YOU** who decides the price of your expertise, time and the course itself.
If you don't think that's worth much, fine, then don't charge much.
But you'll find there are people who prefer paying higher prices for a course.
These people believe they'll be getting a better standard of tuition.
BUT it's up to you to deliver on their expectation.

It's time for some more sums, just to make sure you get the picture.
Your new, well-promoted, course still runs for 35 weeks.
All pay up front so financially it doesn't matter if there's a drop off or not.
So you'll receive $6,000 from ten students who receive the 1/3 discount.

6. PLANNING DIRECTIONS.

Reviewed by: Doug Hill - (Wagga Wagga, Australia.)
1. Sell drawings.
2. What do businesses buy?
3. Have you had an experience like this?
4. Do you complete your painting and then work out how to frame it?
5. Improve the focus and direction of your print marketing.
6. Sell the copyright to your works.
7. Most artists I know don't want to retire.
8. Can you really retire?
9. Retirement is a major career change.

1. Sell drawings

As mentioned already we all have stuff in the too hard basket.
They're good ideas we'll get around to one day.
Maybe they're ideas that seemed good but never quite worked, and so on.
For many artists their too-hard basket contains drawings.

Most artists have been 'brought up' on drawing as a basic artistic skill.
Many artists develop a love of drawing as a consequence.
They continue to draw long after their initial learning period.
It's no surprise to realize that a huge number of drawings have been created.
Some done rapidly as sketches, others are studies for works in other media.
Yet others are very carefully rendered works.
What is a surprise is how hard it is to sell drawings, especially for top money.

However, this should not be a surprise.
The number of drawings means supply exceeds demand, price depressed.
Drawing is also seen as preparatory for a major work and thus lesser.
Because it is common as student work, many drawings are student standard.
So all drawings are seen as inferior.

These statements do not apply to all artists.
However, there are enough potential buyers who think like this.
So artists who wish to sell drawings feel the effect.
If you are one of this group what can you do?

First of all you'll need to accept the sad facts.
You can't get the same return for drawing as you for an equivalent painting.
This has nothing to do with quality of works but to buyer perception of value.
Drawings are seen as low value, paintings higher status and higher value.

This attitude is something that has developed over many years.
It's part of the sociology surrounding art and its marketing.
What can be done if you are a drawer and not very interested in painting?
The approaches suggested will generally help you sell more works.

For many a black and white monochromatic scheme marks drawings.
Apply colour to a drawing; a wash, and the chance of sales increase.
Colour washes are easy to do, even by 'non-painters'.
More importantly, do not obscure the essential drawing.

Drawing in colour is a step further down the track.
Do your actual drawing in coloured pencil, pastel or ink.
Many artists like drawing and use mediums that allow major works.
Which sell for reasonable or even high prices.
For artists in this category painting is not essential at all.

But say you like black and white drawing, as in charcoal or pencil?
Well you can vary this just a little by keeping your work monochromatic.
Sepia works would sell a little better than black and white for example.
They also retain all of the basic drawing character.

What about making your drawings into prints?
This doesn't mean you have to learn etching or lithography, but you could.
Reproduction prints are made easily and cheaply on a photocopier.
Now you have to sell many drawing images rather than just one!
But each print can be sold very cheaply.
The total has the potential to be greater than a single drawing sale could be.

Another idea is to keep your drawings small.
This means less time spent to produce the work and framing is inexpensive.
Prices can be kept down.
It's the expensive drawings that are usually the hardest to sell.

Do you paint as well as draw?
If that's the case, then all of the above suggestions can work for you.
BUT there are some other approaches too.

If most of your drawings are studies for major paintings.
Then they're marketable with the paintings themselves.
Yes, sell the studies with the major work as a package.
Someone buys the work and for an additional sum, also the study.
Exhibit studies at the same time as the major work, but sell for less money.
The presence of the major works will help sell the studies.

You can even give drawings away.
Hey, what's going on here, I can hear you say!

Well the important thing is that you get something for the drawings.
It does not necessarily have to be cash.
For example you could give a study (unframed?) with a painting bought.
What you receive is more money this strategy attracts for paintings.
Which would you rather sell a painting or a study?
Give a framed study to a charity.
Help that organization, get exposure and still have expensive work to sell.
You can even barter studies and sketches for goods (framing?).
If you do enough, it isn't essential to receive high prices for each drawing.

There is one other way you can market drawings too.
Just produce drawings and nothing else.
Make your mark as an artist who draws!
You will draw in a variety of sizes, as a painter does.
Your pricing will reflect the different sizes too.
Then more complex drawings are in larger sizes and attract highest prices.
This is hard at first, but stick to it and sell drawings for reasonable money.

2. What artworks do businesses buy?

A professional artist should make money.
But making money doesn't only mean selling paintings.
Corporations buy all manner of artworks.
Some for boardrooms, large and prestigious works so pay a lot of money.
Business also buy smaller less expensive work for corridors, normal offices.
However, these days most businesses have little money to waste.
They are thus less inclined to buy artworks than a few years ago.

Are there problems for a business that buys artworks?
It may be tax-deductible but the claim is not so easy to substantiate.
Depreciation reduces the attractiveness of this approach to tax minimization.
Depending where you live, there might be a capital gains tax down the track.
This is balanced by the ownership factor.

Could you hire art to businesses, our government here in Australia has.
Artbank, a government institution lends work to government departments.
They also lend art to the non-government sector.
I imagine other countries have similar authorities and arrangements.
To lend artworks on the scale of Artbank requires a huge stock.
Quite a deal of money is invested in their inventory.
Fortunately you don't have to do things on that scale.

Any business that is likely to buy paintings is a candidate for hiring.
The best to approach are those with waiting rooms, boardrooms, and offices.
In other words areas where people sit and look at a blank wall.
Any business that's conscious of its image is a potential hiring client too.

But why hire when you can sell?
By renting or hiring, people pay so much, usually a month, for use of a work.
I had a number of works hired for over 17 years by a firm of lawyers.
Depending how fees are calculated costs can be covered in a year or two.
Everything from then on is pure profit, and you still own the works!

Say someone, who is in business, is contemplating buying a painting.
Hiring can be attractive for a business person so suggest they buy or hire.
It is a legal, tax-deductible expense, if the work is hung at the business.
It's a similar arrangement to hiring cars, or pot plants, or furniture.
The business is paying for the use of these items, but not for ownership.

They're not stuck with the works like they would be if bought outright.
Offer returns (exchange for others) after a period (one, two, six months).
You've a strong argument, and they don't have to worry if a work is criticized.
This is often a concern for people unfamiliar with art.

Business people are used to hiring.
They hire or rent cars, pot plants, furniture, office equipment, etc.
The cost is a legitimate tax deduction too.
My hiring contracts often lasted three or four years.
But many continued longer and less than two years was rare.
As a result of my hiring art to businesses I now own a stock of artworks.
Many are earning me money on a regular basis.

What rental does the business pay?
The simple answer is whatever you convince them to pay.
Fees for hiring link the retail cost of a work to duration of the hiring contract.
I don't tell the client the retail price though.
More recently my fees link the size of the work rather than original cost.

The real cost of hiring is not as great as often thought.
The outlay is reduced by the business's tax rate (which varies).
Tax is claimed for the full hiring fee as it is a legitimate business expense.
It is not reduced by a 'buy-out' figure (as in leasing).

I don't allow any of my hire stock to be bought either.
It's just not part of the arrangement so I don't quote a selling price.
I just say "This work will cost $50 a month (or whatever) to hire.
Other similar works cost the same and some are even less."

You receive passive income from any hiring arrangement.
Passive income is money that arrives at regular intervals.
You need to do little more than set it up.
Receiving rent or dividends are well known forms of passive income.
With enough works hired out, you'll then have a regular income stream.
This irons out the ebb and flow of normal art-world business transactions.
Old unsold work you have (everybody has some) is part of your hire stock.
BUT attract the same hire price, as any other similarly sized new work.
It makes a great deal of sense to do this if it's at all possible.

Arrange annual payments from different clients in different months.
This spreads your income out better.
That will eventually happen anyway.

Offering to exchange works is an important selling point.
Many potential hirers feel they may get tired of the paintings after a while.

They are relieved to know the paintings can be changed.
The longer they keep the works, the less likely they are to change them.
The works become a part of the character of the workplace and its identity.
So frame hired works to match the decor of the business environment.
These works are likely to stay hired for a very long time.
Because they will look as if they belong in that environment.

You can also offer to paint special works to be hired by the business.
Thus you combine commissions, with a corporate approach and hiring.
Commissions have a slightly higher fee than similar non-commissioned work.
Are you likely to get back any work that was commissioned and then hired?
Your descendants will be collecting on this sort of arrangement.

What if the hirer returns the work?
Special frames are in standard sizes so all works fit one or another of them.
Hire returned work out again and there is no cost linked to the work at all.
Profit from day one!

That's also why you wouldn't sell but retain them in your hire stock.
This will save you painting and framing replacements.
If they change works a fee might be the same but the standard could reduce.
BUT it could be altered by starting again with current prices for similar works.
I'd rather add new paintings to my hire stock, instead of replacing ones sold.

Whatever income you earn from hiring just keeps on coming.
It's added to as more businesses hire rather than buy.
This income comes if you go on a holiday and do not paint.
If you are sick and cannot paint or maybe dead the money keeps coming!
Paint works to be hired instead of sold and it's a perfect recipe for retirement.

3. Have you had an experience like this?

A solo show at a local gallery and owe $$$ in spite of two sales?
There is still quite a collection of artworks to sell.
Framing is expensive although they look wonderful hanging at the gallery.
How about trying eBay to move the unsold works?
BUT I want to make 'real' money, not just a few dollars selling junk!
Selling "junk" on eBay is never going to make you rich.
BUT selling cheaply to keep a cash flow without much work makes sense.

The secret to eBay success is using key research tools.
Discover what people are buying and how much they're willing to spend.
If you have a cheap source of product, then sell it at a generous mark-up.
It's not rocket science... and there are no tricks and gimmicks involved.
But you can get a steady, reliable income.
Also there's a chance to grow a huge opt-in list you can sell to in the future.

EBay is an excellent place to do valuable market research too.
Then you know what your potential buyers are buying and why!
It also allows you to grow a huge opt-in list of people you can sell to.
Remember, these are people on the world's largest marketplace.
They're enthusiastic online shoppers!
They're exactly the kind of people you want to introduce your artworks to.

There are artists who swear by eBay.
BUT took them a long time to have a go and furthermore to figure it out!
You can make $500 to $1000 on eBay every week and some artists do.
Sell a low cost item to start with says Mike Barr (Adelaide Australia).
You can sell off unsold works quickly as a way of clearing stock.
Small studies are an ideal beginning too.
Sold unframed they will be easy to pack and ship.
You will be less likely to have negative feedback or DSR's.

Mike has made new works and introduced them on eBay.
There's a whole truckload of painters doing that and enjoying the process.
They are the "daily painters" who work every day on a particular piece.
Once they finish the artwork they post it right away in eBay.
Others paint a small artwork daily so everyday there's a new painting offered.
Reality is you MUST make a profit so sale price – expense = profit / loss.
You should know the price your works are likely to sell for.
Then you will know how much you can spend on production and eBay fees.
EBay's main charges are Insertion Fees and Final Value Fees.

How much risk will you take?
Start **LOW** and you will generate bids **BUT** you **MAY** sell cheaply.
Research complete listing for similar artworks and find out their starting bids?
A lower starting bid attracts a lower initial listing fee.
You are more likely to attract early bidders and get the auction rolling.
Start at the lowest price you accept **BUT** you can turn some bidders away.

Reserve Price strategies.
Down the track you may want to sell your work for a higher price.
Then start the bidding at the lowest price you will take.
Set a Fixed Price and use the Best Offer option to find out what people pay.
The Fixed Price could be higher than you want.

4. Do you complete your painting and then work out how to frame it?

What about if you did things the other way around?
Decide what sort of frame you will use for the painting you are about to do.
This generally means you'll have to make decisions about the work too.
About how big or small will it be?
Roughly what colours will be used?
What kind of tonal scheme will you employ (dark / light and major / minor)?

Do you have any frames that would suit such a painting?
OK then, now paint the painting to fit the frame you have.
If you do not, then order a suitable frame from your supplier.
In this case make sure a frame size fits other works you might do in future.

Many artists equate using conservation materials with professionalism.
They use 100% acid free rag matting and all materials of archival quality.
All paintings are double matted to ensure space and avoid humidity problem.
BUT these are generally more expensive than the alternatives.
A frame can make the work look great or preserve it for 500 years.

For pastel, print and water-colourists there is a choice of glass too.
Non-glare glass is used to avoid light reflected from paintings.
BUT it darkens colour somewhat and underlying art can't be seen as clearly.
UV glass does not seem to affect transparency.

So what is the job of a frame for a professional artist?
Put simply its task is to help you sell the works.
Paintings always look better framed than unframed.
Save on the conservation materials and use what makes the work look best.

Most artists' greatest expense is presentation.
Let's say that is $275 for matting, glass & frame and $50 painting materials.
Your last painting sold for $700 and you only have to pay 20% commission.
After $140 [the 20%] + $9.80 [Tax of 7%] you have $225.60 before tax.
These figures vary greatly depending on the commission rate applying.
Costs are the same whatever price the work but it varies according to size.
Which means there is more actual cash tied up in frames than paintings.

So you should want to sell every frame you have.
Care of frames makes sound business-sense.
There are design factors too!
BUT these are **NOT** cost issues, they are choices!

The very best way to save on framing is to paint smaller.
A small work doesn't cost too much to frame, even elaborately.
It takes more time to cover a large area than small, irrespective of image.
Decreasing the size of your work can increase productivity dramatically.
You get quicker for doing anything well you do it faster than those who don't.
That applies to painting as much as anything else for it's an indicator of skill.

Skill in art, sport or even medicine is basically the same phenomenon.
It's practiced behaviour in action.
Most artists don't do near enough paintings to develop any real skill.

Is there value in smaller works?
In less time you can do more works than previously.
Framing, stretchers, canvas, paper and paint cost less for smaller works.
BUT the frame cost proportion of a selling price is high but low in actual $$$.
So use standard sizes and styles keep the costs down!
Control the size of your works!
Then you control your major costs of production (as distinct from selling).
Select the size of the canvas, paper, board, plate or what you work on first.

By standardizing sizes of your artworks you save money on framing.
If works are the same size only a few actually need to be framed.
You won't need a frame for every painting, only those displayed and on sale.
Then the works can be rotated in the frame from time to time.
More frames are made as sales eventuate.
Thus ten works may only cost you three or four frames to start with.

There is another advantage to standardized frames sizes.
I use four major frame sizes, each of which is ½ or 2x the size of another.
Occasionally I paint an even larger work, which is still in the same proportion.
I don't have many spare frames, but I have unsold work (most are unframed).
It doesn't matter what the actual sizes are, just as long as you stick to them.

About three or four different sizes are sufficient for most artists.
If you work on paper, the frames can be linked to sheet sizes.
The size for full sheet framing, ½ sheet and ¼ sheet covers most artists.
Frames are all in a suitable range of sizes and you can mix and match works.
Eventually you sell all frames, which is where you have actual money tied up.

Standardize your framing style and you'll save even more money.
By retirement you'll know which frames look the best and sell the best too.
For example you always use the same limited range of mat-board colours.
Then buy in greater quantity those colours and get savings from your framer.

5. Improve the focus and direction of your print marketing.

If you make images based on reality or have decorative possibilities.
You can produce prints of these works whenever you want.
You can spend quite a deal of money and time, so avoid expensive mistakes.
Do enough people like your work sufficiently so producing prints is feasible?
If so you have a market you can develop.
It's likely these people will like more than one of your works.
They can become future buyers, provided you know who they are.

Your print marketing objective is sell many works, which are identical.
Selling a painting only needs one person to want a work and agree to price.
If many sales are desired the price is reduced to increase selling chances.
Let's say your paintings usually sell for $1500.
A print for only $30 will obviously attract more people.
Will a price of $15 make even more sales likely?
You don't have to decide straight away, but think along these lines.

People only have limited space on their walls.
So the more works they buy, the less likely it is they'll buy more.
This is a problem if you are planning to sell the same people many works.
That's what a print publisher (you) does.
However small works are more easily placed, as are works clients like.

Plan a suite of prints?
A suite is a number of linked editions.
They'll usually have similar subject matter.
There could be four or six or eight editions.
All will be done to a common theme, in an identical size and presentation.
Produce a suite of flowers, outback landscapes, old pubs, or famous people.
BUT they must be images that appeal to many people.

Then plan the number of prints in each edition of your suite.
So how many of each print will there be **BUT** do **NOT** be ambitious.
It's not rocket science... and there are no tricks and gimmicks involved.
An edition of 1000 might only cost $3 per copy = $3000.
For an extra $500 you print an additional 500 copies saving 40% per copy.
The figures are typical and the principle applies even with different numbers.

But what if we look at that another way?
Don't be too ambitious in terms of expected sales though.
The number of copies available for sale is 500 or 1000.
At the start you have sold none and your basic cost is $2500 or $3000.

When you sell one print it has cost $2500 or $3000.
When you sell two prints each has cost $1250 or $1500.
After the third sale the cost per print is $625 or $750.
You have to sell the lot (500 or 1000) to recover your costs of publication.

Of course you mark your prints up for sale (let's say by 100%)
Now when you sell one print it has cost $1250 or $1500.
When you sell two copies each has cost $625 or $750.
After the third sale the cost per print is $312.50 or $375.
You have to sell half (250 or 500) to recover your costs of publication.
Only then will you start making a profit.

You will start making a profit sooner on a smaller production run.
There are fewer copies to be sold before break-even is reached.
Psychologically, pain of not selling is greater than joy of sales made.
Thus selling the lot is better than having sold few prints.
Smaller production runs are much more likely to sell out than larger runs.
It's not just psychologically better it's, in the long-run, financially better too.

But the hardest part of the whole exercise is making an actual sale.
So people should be pessimistic about the number of sales likely.
Then for production they should cut that in half (at least).
Do not let the printer talk you into more.
The psychological cost of selling those additional prints will be high.
For a first project my suggestion is 50 is the very most you would consider.
It's better to have an edition of 20 sold out, than 495 still to sell.

Decide on the size of your prints.
I suggest small is best with around 30cm x 29cm (12" x 8") is a maximum.
The compact size of each print is designed to make sales easier.
Space for a small print shouldn't give major problems for potential buyers.
Larger prints also require more expensive framing.

BUT a small size contributes to a saleable framed price too.
In fact it may be possible to do a deal with your picture framer for this project.
They will have little wastage when frame sizes are small and identical.
They should be able to pass some of this saving on to you.
It will not cost as much to produce each print in a small size than if bigger.
Several small prints can be produced for the same price as a larger size one.

Do NOT take any notice of a printer who says have more printed.
Do not think in terms of $ per print (which is what they'll do).
Think in terms of $ per sale.

At this point you've sold none.
It's likely you'll sell the same number whether you get 100 or 1000 printed.

Print less than you think you can sell.
Do NOT be ambitious.
Make about half of the number you think is reasonable, or less.
Say you've found a printer who is able to do the job at a reasonable price.
Decide what you can afford.
If you can have the whole suite printed do so.
However it may be necessary to print only one or two images.
In this case select those you think are likely be the most popular to print first.

So now you have some prints.
Probably in one, or maybe two editions of a planned suite.
Here's the really important bit.

ONLY PUT ONE EDITION ON SALE.
Any other editions, keep for the future.

Why do you do this?
Doesn't it mean people have less choice and make sales less likely?
Well, yes and no - it does give people less choice.
They either have to buy the print offered or none.
It is possible you lose sales if people would have preferred one of the others.

BUT it's likely they've bought the one that's for sale.
They didn't know about the others.
So total sales may be down on what they could have been with a choice.
BUT sales of the print available are most likely up on what they could be.
So you'll have less of them left, perhaps even none!

Make the print available for a limited time, and publicized very strongly.
The cut off could be Christmas, next month, Mothers' Day or whenever.
Don't leave a single one up, so you won't be tempted to sell just one more.
If you do that the credibility of your marketing strategy goes out the window.
Make sure you capture the name and email address of each buyer.
This is very important for these people are potential buyers of more prints.
Next year, they can be contacted early by email.

Sales of the second print can be made before they go on public sale.
You could even make special advance offers if you like.
Consequently, you'll sell some (or even many) works to past buyers.
In addition you also sell the next print edition by your marketing system.

This is carried out in the same way as the first year.
Which again means, at a suitable time put the second print edition on sale.
That's after you have satisfied your email clients.

Again make the print available for a limited time.
This is publicized very strongly and the cut off should be the same as before.
Say Christmas, next month, Mothers' Day or whenever.
When that date arrives, remove unsold prints or better they are sold out?
Again you make sure you capture name and email address of each buyer.

You should sell more with two marketing promotions instead of one.
Another advantage of the compact size now becomes obvious.
There are some people you emailed, who wouldn't have otherwise bought.
Now they will create pairs and eventually sets by buying additional prints.
This would be less likely if large prints were sold.
Repeat this process annually with each print edition.
With each new edition there should be a small price rise.
You will probably find that some people are collecting the whole suite.
It is important to publish only a minimal number of prints.
The very best outcome is to sell the lot!
Thus the number printed or published should relate to that probability.
A small number, the more likely that is the outcome (not guaranteed).

6. Sell the copyright to your works.

Copyright is the right to copy an original creative work.
This is not limited to art works, it applies to literature, musical scores as well.
Selling copyright is the main way authors make money from creative work.
Publishers pay for the right to copy the author's story in a book form.
The author keeps the manuscript, or original work.
It has some value, but not as much as the copyright.

Copyright is worth real money, but is seldom exploited by most artists.
Most artists only make money this way if copyright is sold to a publisher.
The publisher will then reproduce copies of the work.
On plates, calendars, as prints, greeting cards, place mats and so on.

BUT it's no easy task to make such a sale.
There's a huge number of artworks produced but we don't know how many.
Of this number, how many have provided money to the artist for copyright?
Not too many in comparison to the number painted, is it?
Not even compared to the number sold!

Most artists receive NO money for this sellable part of art activity.
That's because they think there's only one way to get money for copyright.
That's by selling to a publisher.
There **IS** another way, which you haven't heard about before, anywhere.

Selling the artwork does NOT automatically sell the copyright.
You own the copyright unless it is specifically transferred to someone else.
An artist owns copyright unless it is specifically transferred to someone else.
Ownership gives the legal right to make copies of an original artwork.
It's the right to copy that's owned not necessarily the work itself.
Because someone bought a painting, it doesn't mean they can make cards.

Perhaps you aren't worried about this, for you own the copyright.
You can even produce cards of your paintings, owned by someone else.
A common situation for copyright to be sold by an artist is to a publisher.
The publisher produces prints of the work, in a book or magazine or cards.

When selling copyright, it can be transferred in a limited way.
Sell copyright for a particular image for a certain type of reproduction.
This is NOT for any other kind.
This could mean a publisher has copyright for placemats from a painting.
If they want to produce cards then they must negotiate again.

You can even sell that form of copyright to someone else.
Limitations can also apply in other ways too.

A common limitation is the number to be produced.
The publisher can produce 1000 prints, to do more they must renegotiate.
Geographical limits can also apply.
The prints can only be sold in Australia, London, or where you care to name.
World rights are still to be negotiated.

Selling copyright can be a very attractive proposition.
You may keep the painting, now worth more, and receive income too.
Successful reproduction print artists can be very well rewarded.
You'd be surprised at how well some print artists live, but it is competitive.
An exception is if you are on staff and create a work as part of employment.
Then the employer is the owner of copyright to that work.
Perhaps you are paid as photographer for the local newspaper.
Copyright photographs taken by you in your work is owned by the paper.
If you work freelance then you own the copyright.

Another exception is for the creator of commissioned work.
However this does not apply for say paintings.
A photograph, portrait or engraving created in return for payment (or benefit).
In this case, the client is usually the first owner of copyright.
A third exception is a work was created for, or first published by government.
The government is usually the first owner of copyright, even if it is a painting.
Well you'd expect something like that from government wouldn't you?

It isn't permissible to reproduce one of your works by making changes.
Perhaps by alter the colours, if it's possible to compare the work and a copy.
If important parts of the work can be identified permission to copy is needed.
Even to scan an image on a computer and alter it to a new work.
A copyright owner's permission is needed to copy the image, and to alter it.
Even if is no intention to publish a copy, people still need your permission.
It's about copying rather than what's done with the copy.
It may be OK for art galleries or museums to copy work for archival purpose.

Usually copyright expires on your works 50 years after your death.
This will apply no matter who owns the copyright at that time.
Once copyright has expired it cannot be revived.

There may be more than one copyright to some works.
A photograph of a painting has copyright to the painting and the photograph.
These situations can be changed by agreement between the parties.

A commissioning client may not be the owner of copyright.
But usually entitled to use the work for the reason for which the commission.

They will need the copyright owner's permission for any other purpose.
A publisher commissioned you to paint a series of paintings for place mats.
Cannot just publish prints as well, without your added permission.
Giving the added permission may mean new terms are negotiated.
From all this it follows the owner of a work may not be the owner of copyright.
BUT the owner can sell, exhibit or donate the work, not copyright owner.

It's a good idea for permission to be in writing.
The documentation shows what exactly is covered by the agreement.
You should state you are the owner of copyright.
You don't grant rights to this work to others inconsistent with the agreement.
You could offer compensation if this information is later found to be incorrect.
It costs you nothing, but provides some protection for the copyright buyer.

Describe the work(s) to which copyright is being assigned.
You could supply a copy of the work (photograph) as part of this description.
Set out clearly what you are giving permission for the copyright buyer to do.
You can assign or license just some of the copyright rights.
It's also possible for you to retain some specified rights and sell all else.
You may give exclusive rights or a non-exclusive license.
Set out what is the case.

How long does the permission to copy last?
It may be for the full period of copyright or something less (a sunset clause).
What territory is covered?
It may be local, in Australia or wherever you decide and they agree on.

What do you get?
Set out your payment and/or other benefit you get from this arrangement.
It goes without saying it's a good idea if you receive some benefit from this.
Money is the best benefit, but there are other possibilities.
You should also say when you are to receive this.
On signing the document is best.

Australia is a party to a number of international copyright treaties.
So you're protected in those countries, also parties to those agreements.
For this reason copyright in New Zealand, is much the same as in Australia.
You'll need to check your own country to ascertain if there are differences.

Can you earn money from copyright without publishing at all?
When you sell artworks also have copyright for sale, for a small premium.
Perhaps 10% is a reasonable premium for copyright, but it's up to you.
That's what authors get when they sell copyright.

Sell your painting for $1000 and for an extra $100 the copyright.
It could be the $1100 painting includes $100 for copyright.
Approach whichever way you wish.

Notice you will receive 10% extra income for NO extra work.
Well, not quite, for not all people will want the copyright, but many will.
Whatever the number, it's still extra money just for asking.
It is money you would not otherwise have obtained.
On the other hand the client pays extra and receives something valuable.

You can sell copyright in a limited way too.
Thus you can prevent what you consider to be undesirable promotions.
BUT still obtain money from your asset.
For example the copyright holder may not use your image on a poster.
Limitations may be for a specific number of copies (one, whatever).
There may be geographic limitations to copy sales (no local, within state).
There may be other limitations that you and the potential owner agree on.

Limitations reduce attractiveness for the buyer.
The copyright holder must be able to reproduce your work in some way.
Otherwise they haven't really obtained copyright.

When you sell the limited copyright.
The owner of the painting might have copyright to produce greeting cards.
But for personal use only which are not to be sold.
It's up to you to construct a deal, but there must be an attractive to the buyer.
Otherwise no sale (of copyright at least) will take place.

Don't forget your own copying needs?
There's a particular painting that you would like to make a print of yourself.
Don't let the copyright go or reserve this aspect of copyright for yourself.

What about value adding too?
Selling copyright is a powerful added value factor that brings extra sales.
As well as extra income from each sale for it really costs nothing to try.

What if there's a painting you would like to make a print of yourself?
Don't sell the copyright with this one, or you reserve that aspect to yourself.
Use the ideas suggested in the previous Chapter to produce and your prints.

The more you think along these lines, the more attractive copyright is.
When you retire your values are likely to be at their maximum.
That's the time to sell copyright!
Note your copyright is based on the value of the work.
There's no-one else taking a share.

Selling copyright is a powerful added value factor.
It brings extra sales, as well as extra income from each sale.
Even better, it costs you only a little extra to do.
It's still a little difficult if you can't sell paintings in the first place though.
But that's another matter entirely.

Sell copyright to buyers was in 'Art Professional' 016 for the first time.
It's an idea that, to my knowledge, has never previously been suggested.
And no artist has previously considered.

7. Most artists I know don't want to retire.

Few artists think of retiring.
If they think about it at all it is likely they hope they paint until the last breath.
But retirement **IS** something worth thinking about.
It doesn't necessarily mean you have to stop painting.
But sometimes circumstances make this impossible.
You have an accident, ill health is debilitating, or no-one wants your stuff.
Money must come from somewhere or it's very difficult to live these days.

It's more likely to be that you stop having to earn money by painting.
That's where you started, you painted for fun, satisfaction and pleasure.
If you have enough income then you can do it again if you want to.
You can also give up painting completely if you want to.
It's your choice when you retire.

There is actually something you can do, that most other people can't.
Provided people still want to buy your paintings you can do it yourself.
Yes, you can set up your own superannuation scheme.
But you **MUST** maintain that sales presence.

Some years ago I talked to one of my gallery's artists about this.
My artist was advised to keep all unsold works from any exhibition.
A Sydney gallery owner told him to put them away and forget about them.
For in his old age these paintings would be very valuable.
They'll be the only ones available from the early periods of an artist's career.

People and institutions look for works like these to fill in collections.
Unsold works by the artist will be a similar standard to those that were sold.
Otherwise they would not have been exhibited at all.
The gallery owner didn't suggest inferior unsold works as superannuation.
Inferior works should not be exhibited, let alone kept for the future.

The late Fred Williams is reputed to have had a similar idea.
It's said, every second painting Fred did was put away in a shed.
The others were exhibited, sold and dealt with in the usual fashion.
Those in the shed were Fred's superannuation.
Fred died many years ago and I believe this has been the case.
BUT even if it's not, it still illustrates what's possible.

A few years ago we exhibited Judy Cassab's work.
Judy was then 75 years old and seemed to me to be in good health.

But say this wasn't the case, and she was infirm.
Paintings done earlier in her career can still be exhibited and sold.

Many people are keen to buy an artist's work at this stage in their life.
So there's often a demand for work by elderly artists that cannot be met.
If you've kept sufficient works for this eventuality, then it's possible to cash in.
This could be for your own benefit or relatives and other beneficiaries as well.

Artists named are Australian but no doubt other artists do the same.
The younger you are when you start putting those works away the better.
Be systematic and you can retire in the future if you wish, or must.

There are likely to be taxation aspects to be considered.
But even taking this into account, you have advantages compared to others.
If you declare these works as part of your trading stock.
You'll be required to pay tax on their value at the time they are declared.
This value can be cost of production just the paint, paper, canvas, frame etc.
I believe this is probably what your accountant would advise you to do.
The works are part of trading stock so are not subject to capital gains tax.
In these circumstances you'll not have to pay capital gains tax, years later.
That's when the works are sold, given away, or even bequeathed.

A variation on the above involves work by other artists.
Buy other people's work, or exchange paintings with your artist friends.
There are traps if you broaden your superannuation collection in this way.
You need a gallery to be able to claim other artists' works as trading stock.
Even if you can, you can't claim the cost of production for their value.
It will be whatever you paid but for exchanges it is what you would have paid.
The Tax people are very aware of this aspect.

Superannuation is basically about putting something aside for old age.
In recent years governments encourage people to think of their retirement.
They want people to be in superannuation schemes.
They've even forced employers to provide superannuation for employees.
Government approaches to superannuation are heavy handed and complex.
They are not particularly suited to the needs of artists.
No doubt other governments do similar things often called pension funds.

You can do the right things NOW.
That's much better than wishing you did years down the track.
You can build your retirement income gradually over many years.
Thus there will be a compounding effect.
Much of the retirement plan will benefit your career anyway.

You will have more control over how your career develops.
There will be an orderly development.
Your retirement plan will help you develop a long-term vision for your career.
You will know which opportunities to accept or reject.

Your retirement plan will become your strategic plan.
Then your day to day stuff will fit into that.
Your career will not be subject to random events.
You can harness your reservoir of good will for example.
You will be able to work more effectively with a gallery.
They will appreciate your business-like approach to your career.
That will tend to lead to better gallery arrangements for you.

Retirement is a major career change.
It is best if the approach is planned and systematic.
It's necessary to know where you want to be and also where you are now.
Just as importantly, there needs to be steps for getting from one to the other.
A problem is going from the familiar to something which is not yet known.
We like familiarity.

What happens if you want to retire or when you die?
There will be no more paintings but your business can continue (prints).
Have a clear and transparent plan which suits the circumstances.
You will be giving someone your destiny to look after.
You will probably want this to be nurtured and even further developed.

Who takes over each part of your business?
Estate planning, ownership and divorce are key considerations.
Use a professional to set up protection against a fall-out of death or divorce.
These are major financial road-blocks.
Your plan needs to be open and understood by all - who owns the paintings?

Use the tax system which varies from one country to another.
But generally tax is skewed to growth assets.
Buy property, live in, renovate and then sell or rent.
Some taxes can be paid down the track when the rate is lower.

The first thing to do is to start early, and that means to-day.
There is no earlier time than that to begin the retirement process!
You need to budget wisely and maintain financial discipline.
This doesn't mean just saving money (about 5% to 10% weekly earning),
But investing in growth assets rather than lifestyle (cars, holidays).
AND you **MUST** have a budget.

AND you need cash-flow now!
Without spare money you can't do much.

Basically you will have very limited choices.
Retirement means your financial situation doesn't depend on sales.
Do you want to paint until your last breath to just to keep bread on the table?
Not much of a life is it?
If you retire early you can still paint because that's what you choose to do.
Let's look at what you might have to do in order to retire early.

Match your goals to reality.
If you start early enough you can build your own retirement income source.
BUT be realistic about your current lifestyle and what you can achieve later.
More risk means better returns.
So you invest at a level of risk you're comfortable with (if all goes wrong).
Contrary to much advice don't diversify (spread) but concentrate your risk.
It is best to invest in what you know and understand than what you don't.
You can diversify later if you wish when your capital base has been secured.

When is a change from an active career to retirement considered?
If you have experienced stagnation, then retirement is worth considering.
Outdated products, services, falling sales, and loss of clients are signs.
Other signals are if you feel comfortable and safe, but productivity is low.

But the BEST time to think about retirement is NOW.
The sooner you start a retirement plan the more likely it is that it will happen.
It will also lead to the kind of retirement you actually want.
A long period from commencing your retirement plan and retiring is best.
Then there is time to implement many small steps.
But is having a plan for change enough?
Having a retirement plan is **NOT** enough by itself - that's just a start.

Why is retirement needed and what needs to be done?
The retirement plan and people's tasks and new processes are introduced.
Emotions will be more obvious (apathy, fear, resentment, relief, excitement).
Many hedge their bets and need help understanding a plan & motivation.
How important is it to maintain momentum?
Obviously implementing the retirement plan is the most critical phase.
It is necessary to guard against backing-off.
Like premature declaration of success, wanting to pause for a while etc.
Many people are inclined to finish too soon and give up even sooner.

7. WRAPPING UP.

Reviewed by Mark Wren – (Runway Bay, Australia)
1. Making your art business stand out!
2. What is the nature of development?
3. The ten planning commandments.
4. No plans = no future

1. Making your art business stand out!

It's harder and harder to make a business stand out from the crowd.
There's so much competition for people's attention, they don't take notice.
Recently there was a course on credit card fraud scheduled where I live.
It was cancelled due to lack of interest.
Our local paper castigated local businesses for their lack of interest.
But it's much more likely they didn't even notice it was being held.
It's not enough to say you're doing something and people to pay attention!

Well if you want to be noticed, what works best are the extremes.
Be very radical or very conservative, even old-fashioned.
The middle ground is where failure is these days.
In art that's always been the case!
This reminds of an experience I had back in my art school days.

In my third year of the course, a 'teacher' was different from the rest.
The others had ideas, passed on knowledge, and were keen for us to learn.
They generally did the kinds of things you'd expect teachers to do.
There were slight exceptions, one actually used our work for a book.
Another was keen for us to do well he'd take home unfinished student work.
He'd complete them to ensure a good result (just practicing).
Fortunately this didn't happen to me.

But what about the teacher who was different?
He appeared for his classes and suggested something for us to do.
He had few comments about how we did it or what was done.
Quite often he had been drinking and was not really able to offer much at all.
In addition he regularly arrived late and sometimes left early too.

I was teaching in the outer southern suburbs of Sydney at the time.
I drove in evening peak hour to Darlinghurst, in eastern suburbs of Sydney.
Then drive home near Parramatta in the west each evening.
It certainly was tempting not to come too.
Motivated by an artistic career, I kept turning up for I was trying to learn.

One night, I was the only person there - I had no lecturer to learn from.
I wasn't prepared to waste my time, but I didn't know what to do.

But in two lessons without a teacher I discovered how to get started.
I learned that it doesn't really matter what you do at the start.
The most important thing is to actually do something.
You don't need ideas as once you start, you can alter or change what's done.

It's better to do something and be wrong, than do nothing.
Mistakes can be corrected, and you learn what not to do at the same time.
In addition, your mind works better when there's something for it to work with.
A blank canvas is really uninspiring and even for many people inhibiting.
We are conscious the greatest masterpieces were painted on similar canvas.

Often we try to solve all our problems before we start.
That's generally too hard, usually unnecessary, most worked out on the way.
The new attitude from the hopeless teacher's class I used in all classes.
I learnt from each teacher in my own way and developed my own art.
Importantly I gained self-confidence replacing innocence and naiveté.
Instead of just being diligent, I was passionate and really enjoyed painting.
I continued this attitude into the fourth and final year of my course.

I can recall one of my classmates making a comment to me.
He became a university lecturer with a PHD in Art Education to match.
'It's all right having fun and enjoying yourself, but wait till the end of the year.
You have to do what they want you to do!'
At most educational institutions you do what lecturers want or you fail.

I thought about that briefly, but not for long.
I didn't really care if I passed or failed, for I was on my way to being an artist.
I knew an artist was based on what you did rather than passing a course.
Artists haven't done formal courses, others have failed but it didn't matter!
I kept going as before in spite of the well-intentioned advice from my friend.
I had a busy and productive year and my development moved along well.
I even had two works hung in the Wynne Prize (a major landscape award).
Eventually the end of the year came, and the exams arrived as well.

I received distinctions in every subject!
Naturally I was very pleased and quite proud of the achievement.
A little further down the track I realized what had actually happened.

Thus I learnt another of life's lessons.
The way of examining students was as used in other art institutions.
If the subject was life painting a student submitted works for assessment.
With printmaking a portfolio was required.

The works were viewed by a panel of examiners.
Each was a specialist in the discipline.
One the lecturer but each independently ranked the works from best to worst.
Then the group would compare results for the final mark.

If a marker views works which are all similar but one that is different.
Then the different one will almost always be placed as best or worst.
If some skill and creativity is involved, a best placing is more likely.
If most students have 'done what they wanted you to do'.
Then their works will tend to be similar and somewhat like the lecturers.
This is basically why I received those distinctions.
My work was different from my classmates.
I had to be judged best or worst, but I couldn't possibly be equivalent.
That's how it is in the art world.
If I had been studying medicine, or accountancy.
Then my attitude would have had an entirely different result!

The main point from my experience it was to learn what failure in art is.
It's to be non-remarkable, merely good; do what is expected; or be average.
It's more remarkable to be different or even totally inferior (Eddie the Eagle).
Marketing and promotion are art forms, and have similar principles.
It's up to you whether you want your own art to be remarkable or not.
The principles are exactly the same and apply to an art career to be noticed.
This is the price of fame.
To be memorable, aim at a more remarkable client **EXPERIENCE.**
This is more important than even a better artwork or service (teaching).
Memories of experiences stay in people's minds for a very long time.

2. What is the nature of development?

It is logically impossible to start a process at its conclusion.
For if this was possible, the end-point has already been reached.
Then it cannot be a valid conclusion, or objective.
Then the commencement of the process must be other than that end-point.
Development is movement from a starting point towards an end-point.
The end-point is not necessarily attainable.
This applies particularly to moving towards something more valuable.
Development is direction of growth by some means, to something of value.
The value is thought to result from the means.

Progression is another term for development.
In human activity development can be movement towards ideal behaviour.
Development takes place as an individual finds and accepts limits.
The limits are imposed by heredity, experience, the environment, etc.
Along with improved understanding of the limiting factors.
They are able to move harmoniously with them.
Discipline is a balance of external limits and internal freedom.
The freedom is of thought and emotion.
The balance is achieved by the responsible exercise of freedom within limits.
With a growing breadth of the limiting factors.

Development involves changes of an irreversible nature over time.
Something that can return to its original state hasn't developed.
An educated person has these values or a few of the highly ranked values.

Performance of a task is related to practice at that task.
This might be mounting an exhibition or retiring from your artistic career.
Initially it is uncontrolled and the results unpredictable.
People beginning watercolour will know what this means.
With more practice comes control and we can predict what might happen.
Our past experience is the basis for this.

As we practice even more, we become more effective.
Results improve as we avoid what leads to mistakes and unwanted outcome.
Most successful galleries work at this level as a result of years of experience.
It seems easy to the observer.

The earlier your retirement plan commences the better it will become!

.
                                                  Flexible

.
                                               Responsive

Performance

.
                                  Effective

.
                                  Efficient

.

.
                           Control

.
                           Predictable

.

.
                Uncontrolled

.
                Unpredictable

.... *Practice*

Where is your career on this scale?

At the highest level there's a flexibility of performance.
The artist can respond to any situation because of their experience.
Someone can paint portraits, not just pictures of people, for example.
In your retirement situation, you can deal with anything that comes along.

3. The ten planning commandments.

Planning commandment 1: Define your goals:

Just where do you want to get to and why are you doing this?
Are they short term (immediate), medium (this year), or long (five years)?

Short-term objectives:
Sell paintings right away, or get exposure you've not had or similar.
If you need money then that will be a short-term objective.

Medium term objectives:
Become established in a specific gallery, or be a portrait painter.
Long term objectives:
Along the lines of being able to obtain a regular income from your painting.

Don't bite off more than you can chew.
Make your short-term objectives stepping stones towards the long-term ones.
Then you are more likely to be successful.
Or else short-term objectives, are more pressing, and take precedence.

Planning commandment 2: Evaluate the mathematics:

What constitutes success in terms of money?
How much will you need and can you make this much?
How many works will you sell and what will their average price need to be?
Compare alternative methods of selling.
If you sell from a studio how does this compare with hiring exhibition space?
Compare advertising on TV with newspapers, and so on.
If you have a print project look at alternative ways for prints to be made.
Consider a publisher, photocopy, enlarged photographs, etc.
Establish your likely marketing expenses.
How much for mailing, printing, advertising, refreshments, commission, etc.?
Take everything into account - how will you sell the paintings or prints?

Evaluate your response needs.
What sort of response do you really need to make this project worthwhile?

Planning commandment 3: Define your communication needs:

The artwork.
How do you communicate about this in terms potential clients respond to?
It isn't easy to see creative work in a way that appeals to possible buyers.

But unless you do there's likely to be few sales.
What sort of people are you trying to reach anyway?
Are they old or young, male or female and what income bracket?
How can you categorize the market to reach those people?

Action needed will be determined by answers to the above questions.

Planning commandment 4: Define the strategy:

You have a choice of media and lists.
The media varies: paper, mail, phone, TV, letterbox drops, signs on a car.
Probably you'll need to use more than one method.
If you are mailing or telephoning, then you'll need a list of people to contact.
The very best people are your past buyers.
People like them and those who say they will buy being the next best.
Techniques used vary widely.
Here you decide exactly how your ad or invitation or print brochure will look.
Response mechanisms are devices for enticing some sort of action.
Coupons returned, numbers called, gifts collected, or other ways.

Planning commandment 5: Define 'life cycle' and database strategies:

How long will your work stay current?
If at the start of a professional journey it's an important question.
If your work varies widely then people may worry.
What they've bought might no longer be available next time around.
How soon do you want to sell prints?
What will happen after that?
Will you be collecting people's names now so you have a database later?

Planning commandment 6: Develop a test plan:

Test everything, obviously that's not possible so where to start?
Start with marketing most likely to affect the outcome, mailing list, media etc.
If you test in small samples it may save wasting a lot of money later.

Your artwork and framing should be tested too.
Show different possibilities to likely and past buyers and see their reaction.
Use the same way with people who haven't bought – any different reactions.
Test your creative strategy too.
How will you go about marketing an exhibition rather than what is on show?
For example try different invitation layouts and show them to different groups.
The offer strategy is important and should be tested so you use the best way.

It's amazing how different return coupon positions can affect the result.
Timing is hard to test in the short term, but is critical.
Launch a new print at different times in different places to assess the result.

Planning commandment 7: Define back end + resources needed:

A 'back-end' strategy is something to follow up and capitalize on.
Say you've some prints for sale.
Do whatever is necessary to sell them and that's the front (obvious) end.
The back-end is available as you know potential buyers of original works.
Making sales of paintings to these people would be a back-end strategy.
This is potentially more lucrative than the front-end.

Planning commandment 8: Monitor systems to measure responses:

How will you know you've been successful?
Will it be sales, number of people inquiring, or what?
To determine success you need to compare something with something else.
Will it be the ratio of sales to inquirers?
Perhaps the number of sales this time compared with last time.
Another measure may be $ earned now compared with a previous occasion.
Information you gather this time is used as a base for future assessments.

Planning commandment 9: Gain cooperation fully inform everyone:

People can't cooperate with you if they don't know what is going on.
Do not assume everyone knows what is expected - make sure they know.
Gallery owner, mother, husband, helps if they know what they have to do.

Planning commandment 10: Be creative:

Now that shouldn't be too hard should it?
If you have all the planning out of the way and know where you are going.
Then you can become creative about how you'll do it.
The basic structure of your plan will give you something to work with.

4. No plans = no future

Most artists have some semblance of an artistic or a business plan.
It's usually in a few vague ideas on direction and anticipated earnings.

Career planning is the process of developing a map towards the future.
To reach a desired destination, a map must be clear, accurate, easy to use.
Clarity: is achieved through intensive analysis.
Accuracy: is achieved by repeated application and fine-tuning.
Ease of use: the more you use your plan the easier it gets.

To achieve this level of plan you may need to re-think your career.
Your success is entirely dependent on embracing the importance of planning.
You must believe it can be done, hassle free, easily and quickly.
Then you move from:
Think, do, do, evaluate, do, think, think, do, think, scratch, panic, think, do, frustration. Do, think.

With proper career planning to:
Think, think, think, think, do, do, do, do, do, evaluate, evaluate.

Your actions can now become effective.
Everyone does the right things at the right time so you control what happens.
You have a longer term vision about your career than most artists do.
Artists tend to focus on an individual painting.
What if the focus is on the exhibition, as one of a series of exhibitions?
That's what a successful artist does and then there's a different mind-set.
The initial steps of a professional career is an extension of this thinking.
The early days of your career determine how successful you are likely to be.
Take time, establish the fundamental building blocks and success comes!
You are doing this or you wouldn't be reading this career guide.
BUT the odds **ARE** still stacked against success.

Your work being good enough is just the start!
Blend your unique style with a chance of earning a reasonable income?
Develop your own style of painting which may or may not generate income.
Develop efficient work habits to maximize productivity and potential income.
You develop professional knowledge and enter the professional ranks.
Now generate income and profit.

Students
Generally hobby and semi-professional artists.
Occasionally professional artists.

Format
Week-end (2 days)
Lunch & morning/afternoon tea each day.
No enrollment after (close date)
No extra materials to be bought.
Maximum might be 15 whilst the minimum is the break/even number.
Do things regularly e.g. at Easter, Xmas, end of financial year, etc.
Include research component so you learn something each time.

Incentives:
Free Report for early bird enrollers.
Extra Discount for special groups (you decide).
Leverage schools, magazines, art societies and other groups.
Sell before course (e.g. at this course pay for the next one) at reduced price.
Up-sell future courses (block of 4 for price of 3)
Add-Ons - art materials
Cross-sell Reports, tapes, videos, artist's prints, art supplies, etc.

Follow Up:
Questionnaire after course.
Mailing list now for future so can sidestep societies, schools, etc.

Collect all money up front.
Standard price for all courses.
$150 per person for both days.
No extra materials to be bought.

Discounts
If paid by early bird date ($100)
Pay for next course at reduced price
Future courses (block of 4 for price of 3)
10% for group of 5 or more book together.
Kickback for people who get others to attend

Add-Ons
Free Report for early bird
Gift art materials from your stock
Lunch & morning/afternoon tea

Extras
Accommodation
Out of town students stay at same venue.
Teacher stays at venue (arrange a contra deal with accommodation) for you
or someone else.

What do students receive?
Tuition
Written course notes
List materials needed

Discounts
If paid by early bird date ($100)
Pay for next course at reduced price
Future courses (block of 4 for price of 3)
10% for group of 5 or more book together.
Kickback for people who get others to attend.

Free
Report for early bird
Artist's story (you or teacher).
Gift art materials from your stock
Lunch & morning/afternoon tea

Extras
Accommodation
Out of town students stay at same venue.
Teacher stays at venue (if contra deal)

What does a teacher get (you or someone else)?
Artist
Stress importance of actual teaching ability as well as artistic ability.
Standard artists payment
For all courses.
$500 for artist (flat fee any number of students to 15)
No other fee, no expenses
You pay all expenses
Stay with you if contra deal not organized

Supplies
'My Story' which is their own story.
Course notes and materials needed with alternatives
Who would benefit from this course?
commonsense advice
professional tuition
practical help
or whatever.

What you need to do (even if not the teacher)?
Develop mailing lists
High schools
Art societies
Art teachers
Artists as attendees

Write and print literature.
Headings **MOST** important
Focus on factors that qualify the client (sort them out).
Pre-sales literature.
Designed to contact people who would benefit most from this course.
Focus on what's in it for them, which are the benefits.
Be specific ... which means that .. (key benefit).
Value factors. (training, skill, commitment, status, their investment, testimonials.
Say how you'll meet their needs.
Use photographs and cartoons.

State offer
Assume everyone is interested and will come.

Call for action
Tell people what to do.

After-sales literature
Similar to pre-sales literature
Except, designed to help student explain to others, answer questions, adds to knowledge
.
Double check everything to make sure this is what you do.

SUPPORT:

Australian Artist magazine – magazine for Australian artists

International Artist magazine – magazine for artists

Clipping Path Universe – for photo-shop editing

Cherri Computers – computer hardware, software and printers

WHERE NEXT:

BUT being a professional artist is NOW harder than it ever was.
There are other books that link with this book.
You might need one or more of them:

PRICE RIGHT - Then sell.
http://www.amazon.com/dp/B087S85HS8

PLANNING – Means Success
http://www.amazon.com/dp/B087SCD1NY

CAREER BASICS
http://www.amazon.com/dp/B087SCJYX3

FINDING BUYERS - How?
http://www.amazon.com/dp/B087SM58GJ

FIRST WEBSITE - Simple is best.
http://www.amazon.com/dp/B087SFZ6RD

SUCCESSFUL SELLING - Learn how.
http://www.amazon.com/dp/B087SHDKPN

FRAMING = helps sales
http://www.amazon.com/dp/B087SGS6MB

CHRISTMAS - Special approaches.
http://www.amazon.com/dp/B087SHDKPN

TAKE THE PLUNGE - become professional
http://www.amazon.com/dp/B087SFTD61

PRODUCTIVITY – the foundation
http://www.amazon.com/dp/B087S87HLD

COPYRIGHT - making money from copyright sales.
http://www.amazon.com/dp/B0892HWYTV

NOT NOW:

Perhaps one of these books could interest you then?

Write about your own memories.
http://www.amazon.com/dp/B087DWKPTP

A simple way to start developing creativity.
If you are a parent, teacher or someone who meets a group regularly?
http://www.amazon.com/dp/B088T1KFQZ

Here is how most people start becoming an artist!
http://www.amazon.com/dp/B088Y1DPL6

More of my memories.
http://www.amazon.com/dp/B088Y4RPL9

Start an art career but it's **NOW** is harder than it ever was.
http://www.amazon.com/dp/B088T7VJ76

SEND TO:

Know anyone interested in chocolate recipes?
Then send them this link.

http://www.amazon.com/dp/B088Y4RPL9

Know anyone interested in THIS book?

http://www.amazon.com/dp/B087SCD1NY